MW01443619

EMPOWERING ENGLISH LEARNERS

A Comprehensive Guide for ESL Teachers, Parents and Children

Copyright © 2024 Brenda

All rights reserved. No part of this publication may be reproduced, distributed, or transmitted in any form or by any means, including photocopying, recording, or other electronic or mechanical methods, without the prior written permission of the copyright holder, except in the case of brief quotations embodied in critical reviews and specific other noncommercial uses permitted by copyright law. This content is provided for informational purposes only and does not constitute financial, legal, or professional advice. The author and publisher shall not be liable for any loss or damage arising from using the information contained in this publication.

DEDICATION

To my son and daughter, you inspire me every day to keep pressing forward and write my story! I love you both so much!

To my mom and sisters, you choose to stay by my side no matter what, and I am forever grateful.

To my Earth Angel, you taught me to be courageous and open to what love and adventures can be like. Thank you!

My inspiration comes from the people I love most in my life. Thank you for being present! PRESENT means GIFT, so the present "now" in time is a gift!

A NOTE FROM THE AUTHOR

Life is like a book, and we're the author of it. So many chapters of my life have closed, but I know deep inside that there are many more chapters to be written in my book. These chapters in my book included the utmost joy when I became a mother to my two children, the most profound sadness when I lost people, complete tiredness and anger when I was betrayed and lost trust in what I once thought was so good for me, and unconditional love with the people that chose to stay. Every day I'm with my children; they remind me that I am the author of my story, and I get to decide what to write in it. Love is a choice. Being a good role model for them and the future generation is a choice!

Life is a series of pivotal moments that shape us into who we become. Among my most significant life events are the separation of my parents and the incredible journey my mother embarked upon as a single parent, raising my sisters and me. This transition not only marked a new chapter but also laid the foundation for the values I hold dear today.

I was born in Hong Kong with my two older sisters. I come from a big family with lots of relatives, but at age nine, my parents decided to move to America, where I grew up and went to school. I quickly adapted to the culture and began my early years of education learning a new language. My mother's family has resided in the US for over a century, so we are deeply rooted here in my hometown.

After we moved to America, my parents separated, and my mother raised us three girls alone. She instilled in us the belief that we should always be self-reliant, encouraging my sisters and me to find our voices and stand firm in our convictions.

After we moved to America, my parents separated, and my mother raised us three girls alone. She instilled in us the belief that we should always be self-reliant, encouraging my sisters and me to find our voices and stand firm in our convictions. I learned not to rely on others for my happiness and to value my individuality. When faced with challenges, whether they were academic, social, or emotional, I approached them with a sense of determination and resilience, understanding that growth often accompanies discomfort.

Despite my strong sense of independence, I came to realize the beauty of connection. I opened my heart to the possibility of welcoming soulmates and genuine friendships. Life taught me that people are transient; some enter our lives for a brief moment, while others become enduring sources of support and joy. I learned to cherish those who choose to stay, viewing each relationship as a blessing that adds richness to my journey.

I have always been very driven, and in my young adulthood, I worked diligently to get into a graduate program where I obtained my doctorate degree and had the opportunity to specialize in pediatrics. I love working with children, and my passion has always been with them. Prior to that, I was an elementary education major in college and then decided to go into the medical field. I obtained my doctorate degree in my early 20s and got married in the same year that I plunged into my new career at the hospital. Three years later, we got pregnant with my son, and my daughter came two years after that.

All it took was just one second, one moment, and everything changed. I entered a season of my life when I needed and chose to change my career to be with my children. They needed me, and I needed them. And that's when I went back to the education field, teaching English to students globally. This was the right decision that led me on a path to success where I got the opportunity to build my business based on something I'm passionate about, and it doesn't feel like work. I get the honor to make an impact in peoples' lives every time I teach. Children bring hope and strength, so they are actually making an impact in my life at the same time!

Throughout my life, I've faced losses—whether in relationships or in the choices I've made. Each disappointment left a mark, but with time, I recognized these moments as catalysts for growth. They taught me resilience, adaptability, and the significance of learning from my mistakes. With every setback, I gained wisdom and clarity, shaping my understanding of love, loyalty, and what it means to connect with others truly.

When one door closes, another one opens. My determination and resilience kept me pressing forward to be a good role model for my son and daughter. They keep me grounded, honest and light-hearted. I wake up every day pushing myself to be the better version of ME and never to feel stuck. As I continued my English teaching career during those years, I felt hopeful and empowered to help others in another way that I never knew existed.

I started to gain consistent booking from my students and parents, and they started requesting me to teach their children on a weekly basis. What I was doing in the classroom was working, and students loved it, and so did their parents. Then, I realized that this could be an excellent start to fulfilling my dream of being an entrepreneur and combining it with my skills in education and passion for working with children. The consistent flow of new students and the demand grew over time, and I saw the opportunity to invest in myself. This is how my online school was formed. (no duplications.)
I wanted to give families opportunities to learn English just like I did when I was young. I wanted a place for parents to know that this is a program that's going to help their children be successful because we authentically care and have an excellent track record with hundreds of learners just like them.

Over the years, I've had the privilege of teaching over 3,000 students from diverse countries and delivering more than 20,000 online English classes as a TESOL-certified teacher. I use a curriculum developed from high-quality materials aligned with the CEFR standards, designed to meet the varied needs of learners worldwide. Additionally, I serve as a mentor to our dedicated team of teachers, fostering growth and collaboration within our expanding community of educators. Balancing my roles as an educator, leader, and mother is a rewarding journey that continues to inspire my commitment to language education.

My experiences have empowered me to embrace both my strength and vulnerability. I no longer fear the unknown or the potential for heartbreak; instead, I greet it with curiosity and courage, knowing that each interaction holds the potential for growth as a professional, mother, and individual. I am learning every day, no matter what age. I believe that if I can at least touch one life, one student from one experience, then I have done my job as a teacher, a coach, and a leader. It is all worth the while!

I believe that learning a language is learning for life. It is a tool that the learners will always have. English as a Second Language (ESL) is an investment that has excellent value no matter where you live. Imagine the doors that will open knowing English, a widely used language, to possibly get into the school of your choice when it's competitive. Maybe the children can study abroad and experience something extraordinary, immersing themselves fully in the language. Whatever the personal goals may be for the teachers, parents, and students, I have the pleasure of helping many reach their goals. That is very rewarding!!

My significant life events have shaped a story of resilience, loyalty, and an appreciation for the connections that enrich our lives. The lessons learned through challenges and relationships have equipped me with the tools to navigate life's uncertainties. Each chapter adds depth to my narrative, and as I continue to grow, I look forward to the unfolding journey ahead—one filled with opportunities for love, growth, and self-discovery.

It is my mission to share my knowledge, experience, and resources with as many students and parents as possible. My future aspiration also includes providing English classes to young learners in countries where resources are limited and offering more opportunities for children to learn phonics, grammar, speaking, and writing, and an approach that helps them apply the skills gained in our English classes to express themselves more confidently and effectively!

Table of Contents

DEDICATION iii

A NOTE FROM THE AUTHOR iv

INTRODUCTION 1

   My Journey as an ESL Teacher 1

   The Crucial Role of Parents in ESL Learning 2

   A Practical Guide for the ESL Community 4

- Chapter 1 - 11

UNDERSTANDING THE BASICS OF ESL LEARNING 11

   Defining ESL and Its Global Significance 11

   Navigating ESL Challenges: A Roadmap for Parents ... 13

   Creating a Language-Rich Home Environment 16

- Chapter 2 - 20

THE ROLE OF TEACHERS IN ESL EDUCATION 20

   The Critical Role of Teachers in ESL Education 20

   Teaching Environments and Essential Skills for ESL Educators 23

   Effective Communication Strategies between Teachers, Parents, and Students 28

   Supporting Language Development Outside the Classroom 32

- Chapter 3 - 36

THE ROLE OF PARENTS IN ESL EDUCATION 36

   The Critical Role of Parents in Their Child's ESL Education ... 36

Effective Communication Strategies Between Teachers,
　　Parents, and Students 39

　　Ways Parents Can Actively Support Their Child's Language
　　Development Outside the Classroom 43

- Chapter 4 - 49

BUILDING A STRONG FOUNDATION IN ENGLISH LANGUAGE 49

　　Key Aspects of English Language Learning 49

　　Classroom Activities and Resources for Teachers 51

　　At-Home Activities and Resources for Parents 53

　　Common ESL Mistakes and Teacher Strategies 56

　　Common ESL Mistakes and Parent Strategies 59

- Chapter 5 - 62

TAILORING LEARNING STRATEGIES TO YOUR STUDENT'S OR CHILD'S NEEDS 62

　　The Importance of Understanding Learning Styles and
　　Preferences 62

　　Identifying Strengths and Weaknesses in English Language
　　Learning 64

　　Personalized Strategies for Different Types of Learners 67

- Chapter 6 - 72

USING TECHNOLOGY TO ENHANCE ENGLISH LANGUAGE LEARNING 72

　　Benefits of Incorporating Technology into ESL Education 72

Recommended Online Tools, Apps, and Resources 75

Safely Navigating the Online Learning Landscape 78

- Chapter 7 - 82

FOSTERING A LOVE FOR READING AND WRITING IN
ENGLISH 82

The Importance of Reading and Writing Skills in Mastering
English Language Proficiency 82

Engaging Reading Materials and Writing Prompts for Different
Proficiency Levels 85

Tips for Parents to Cultivate a Love for Reading and Writing in
Their Child 87

- Chapter 8 - 92

OVERCOMING CHALLENGES AND CELEBRATING
PROGRESS 92

Common Roadblocks for ESL Learners and Their Parents 92

Practical Solutions and Strategies for Overcoming Challenges 94

Celebrating Small Victories and Milestones 97

- Chapter 9 - 100

CREATING A SUPPORTIVE LEARNING COMMUNITY 100

The Importance of Building a Supportive Network 100

Tips for Connecting with Other ESL Families 103

Guidance on Seeking Additional Support 106

- Chapter 10 - 110

FOR PARENTS - NURTURING YOUR CHILD'S ENGLISH VOCABULARY 110

    The Power of Shared Reading..111

    Gamifying Vocabulary Learning 112

    The Art of Visual Learning 113

    Embracing Technology for Vocabulary Enhancement............114

    The Power of Personal Connection 114

    Celebrating Progress and Maintaining Motivation.................115

    The Importance of Consistent Exposure 116

    Leading by Example 116

- Chapter 11 -...118

DAILY ROUTINE IN HOW TO BE SUCCESSFUL LEARNING ENGLISH 118

    The Power of Routine in Language Learning 118

    Engaging Daily English Routine for Children 119

    Morning Rituals for English Immersion 120

    Maximizing English Exposure Throughout the Day................121

    Evening Routines for Reflection and Consolidation with Children..123

    Weekends and Free Time: Balancing Structure and Fun for Young Learners 124

    Adapting Your Routine for Different Life Stages and Circumstances 125

    Overcoming Challenges and Staying Motivated.....................126

The Long-Term View: Building a Lifestyle of English Learning 127

- Chapter 12 - 129
FUN ONE-TO-ONE ENGLISH TEACHING GAMES FOR PARENTS AND TEACHERS OF ESL 129

The Power of Play in Language Learning 129

Vocabulary-Building Games 130

Grammar Games 131

Pronunciation and Speaking Games.. 132

Listening Comprehension Games.. 133

Reading and Writing Games.. 134

Adapting Games for Different Proficiency Levels 135

Creating a Positive Gaming Environment 136

Integrating Games into Regular Learning Routines 137

The Long-Term Impact of Game-Based Learning................... 137

CONCLUSION 139

The Tapestry of ESL Education: Key Takeaways and Parental Involvement 139

The Ongoing Journey: Practicing English Together and Embracing Lifelong Learning 142

A Note of Gratitude: Celebrating Your Commitment to the English Language Journey... 145

INTRODUCTION

All these years of teaching the English language online surely make me feel privileged to have been able to pursue this amazing journey taken up by both young and adult learners in learning the language. It is a journey full of challenges, triumphs, and "aha!" moments never to leave my face without a smile. However, over time, I came to feel that the real essence of ESL teaching cannot boil down to such a huge amount of lists of vocabulary and grammar rules. It all boils down to an issue of merely creating that very type of environment where the language will grow and flourish on its own.

My Journey as an ESL Teacher

I still remember the feeling of my first day as an ESL teacher; fresh in my mind, it somehow feels as if it was yesterday. I went in with a lot of eagerness, a set of lesson plans, and a will to do some good. Little did I know that my students would teach me much, just the same as I would teach them.

Vivian was one of my first students: a 7-year-old quiet girl. At first, she would not utter a word louder than a whisper; she never looked away from her desk. But over the weeks, she literally came out of her shell. I remember her raising her hand to answer a question on her own without prompting. It wasn't just the English she was learning; it was confidence.

It is experiences like these that have shaped my approach to teaching English. I know that each student travels a different path, and our job as teachers is to guide that journey, urging them forward and sometimes catching them when they stumble. It is not always easy; it is gratifying.

And in due time, I found my toolkit of strategies that goes beyond the traditional textbook learning: we sing songs, we act out stories, we play word games, and sometimes we just have good old-fashioned conversations about anything and everything because that's what language is really all about - connection, communication.

But probably the most important thing that I have come to learn is the fact that learning does not just stop with that sound of the ringing bell. This brings me to the heart of this guide.

The Crucial Role of Parents in ESL Learning

If there's one thing I've observed time and time again, it's that the students who thrive the most are those whose parents are actively involved in their language-learning journey. It's like trying to grow a garden - you can plant the seeds in the classroom, but with nurturing at home, they will reach their full potential.

I'll never forget the day one of my adult students, a dedicated mother named Alice, approached me after class. She confessed that she felt helpless watching her son struggle with English learning since it is their second language at home. "I want to help," she shared, "but I don't know how." That conversation was a turning point for me. It made me realize that we need to empower not just our students but their families as well.

Parents are their children's first and most influential teachers. They have a unique opportunity to create an English-rich environment at home, turning everyday moments into learning opportunities. From reading bedtime stories to discussing the day's events at dinner, these small interactions can have a massive impact on a child's language development.

But here's the thing - many parents feel overwhelmed or ill-equipped to support their child's English learning, especially if they need more confidence in their English skills. That's why it's crucial to bridge the gap between the classroom and home, providing parents with the tools and confidence they need to be active participants in their child's language journey.

Throughout my career, I've seen incredible transformations when parents become engaged in the process. There was the mother who started learning English alongside her daughter, turning it into a shared adventure. The father began incorporating English words into their daily routines, making it a fun family game. These parents didn't just support their children's learning - they inspired them.

Of course, it can be challenging sailing. I've had heart-to-heart conversations with parents who feel frustrated or discouraged. But I always remind them that language learning is a marathon, not a sprint. Every small effort counts, and consistency is vital. It's about creating a positive attitude towards English, making it a natural part of family life rather than a chore to be endured.

That's why I'm so passionate about creating resources that empower parents. When we equip parents with the right tools and knowledge, we're not just helping one child—we're potentially impacting generations to come.

A Practical Guide for the ESL Community

This book is the result of countless conversations, observations, and "light bulb" moments accumulated over years of teaching. It's not just a theoretical approach to ESL learning—it's a collection of real-world strategies, tried and tested in classrooms and living rooms around the world.

My goal is to create a comprehensive resource that speaks to everyone involved in a child's ESL journey - teachers, parents, and the children themselves because successful language learning is truly a team effort.

For teachers, you'll find innovative lesson ideas, tips for creating an inclusive classroom environment, and strategies for engaging even the most reluctant learners. I'll share some of my favorite activities that have turned mundane grammar lessons into exciting adventures and offer advice on how to tailor your approach to different learning styles and cultural backgrounds.

Parents, this guide is your roadmap to supporting your child's English learning at home. We'll explore simple yet effective ways to incorporate English into your daily routines, from cooking together to exploring your neighborhood. You'll find suggestions for age-appropriate books, apps, and games that make learning fun. Most importantly, we'll address common concerns and challenges, providing you with the confidence to be your child's most prominent language-learning ally.

I've included a special section for the young learners themselves, filled with engaging activities, puzzles, and stories designed to spark their curiosity and make English come alive outside the classroom.

But this book is more than just a collection of tips and tricks. It's an invitation to join a community of learners, teachers, and parents who are all working towards the same goal—helping children thrive in their English language journey.

Throughout these pages, you'll find real stories from ESL families and teachers around the world. These anecdotes serve as both inspiration and practical examples of how others have overcome challenges and celebrated successes. Because sometimes, knowing you're not alone in your struggles can make all the difference.

Learning a new language is about more than mastering grammar and vocabulary. It's about opening doors to new cultures, perspectives, and opportunities. It's about building confidence and fostering a love for lifelong learning. Most importantly, it's about empowering children to express themselves and connect with others in an increasingly globalized world.

So whether you're a seasoned ESL teacher looking for fresh ideas, a parent embarking on this journey for the first time, or a student eager to improve your English skills, I hope this guide will be your companion and cheerleader along the way.

As we go into the chapters ahead, I invite you to approach this journey with an open mind and a spirit of adventure. There will be challenges, of course, but there will also be moments of joy, laughter, and incredible pride as you watch English skills blossom.

Let's embrace the ups and downs, celebrate the small victories, and support each other every step of the way. Because when it comes to learning English, we're all in this together. So grab a cup of tea (or coffee, if you prefer!), get comfortable, and let's embark on this exciting ESL journey together.

I want to share a little mantra that has guided me throughout my teaching career: "Live, Laugh, Love, and Learn." These four words encapsulate the essence of what language learning should be. It's about living the language, not just studying it. It's about finding joy and laughter in the process, even when faced with challenges. It's about fostering a love for the language and the cultures it represents. And, of course, it's about continuous learning - not just for our students but for us as teachers and parents, too.

Learning is an everyday process, no matter what age we are. I've had seven-year-old students teach me slang I'd never heard before, and I've watched grandparents pick up English alongside their grandchildren, proving that it's always possible to start. This journey we're on isn't just about reaching a destination - it's about growing, evolving, and discovering new aspects of ourselves along the way.

As we explore strategies and techniques in the coming chapters, please keep an open mind and be willing to experiment. What works brilliantly for one learner might fall flat for another, and that's okay. The beauty of language learning is that there's no one-size-fits-all approach. It's about finding what resonates with you and your learners and being willing to adapt and evolve your methods as you go.

I also want to acknowledge that this journey can be challenging. There will be days when motivation is low, when progress seems slow, or when cultural misunderstandings lead to frustration. In those moments, it's crucial to remember that we're never truly stuck. Every challenge is an opportunity for growth, and sometimes, the most significant breakthroughs come right after the most formidable obstacles.

Throughout this guide, you'll find not just techniques and activities but also stories of resilience, creativity, and the incredible human capacity for learning. These stories come from my own experiences, from fellow teachers I've had the privilege of working with, and from the brave students and families who have shared their journeys with me.

There's the story of a refugee student who arrived in my class unable to speak a word of English. Through sheer determination and the support of his classmates, he went from silent observer to class presenter in just one school year. Or Steven and Shan, hard-working parents who learned English alongside their daughter, turning their evening homework sessions into a bonding experience that strengthened both their language skills and their relationship.

These stories remind us that language learning is so much more than verb conjugations and vocabulary lists. It's about breaking down barriers, building connections, and opening up new worlds of possibility.

As we progress into the practical aspects of ESL teaching and learning, please keep these human stories in mind. At the end of the day, that's what this is all about—helping real people communicate, express themselves, and achieve their dreams.

In the chapters that follow, we'll explore a wide range of topics crucial to ESL success. We'll look at creating immersive language environments both in the classroom and at home. We'll discuss the importance of cultural awareness and how to navigate the sometimes tricky waters of cross-cultural communication. We'll delve into the latest research on language acquisition and how we can apply those findings in practical, everyday situations.

For teachers, we'll explore classroom management techniques that foster a supportive learning environment, even with students of varying skill levels. We'll look at how to incorporate technology effectively, balancing the benefits of digital tools with the irreplaceable value of face-to-face interaction. We'll also discuss strategies for assessment that go beyond traditional tests to measure a student's growing communication skills truly.

Parents will find guidance on how to support their child's language learning without adding stress to their already busy lives. We'll explore fun family activities that naturally incorporate English, from cooking international recipes to planning imaginary vacations.

You'll learn how to create a language-rich home environment, even if you need more confidence in your English skills. And we'll address common concerns, like how to handle homework struggles or what to do when your child seems to be losing motivation.

For students, whether children or adults, we'll provide strategies for making English a part of your daily life. From finding English-language media you genuinely enjoy to practicing with language exchange partners online, you'll discover ways to immerse yourself in the language that you don't feel like studying.

Throughout it all, we'll emphasize the importance of maintaining a positive attitude and celebrating progress, no matter how small. Learning a language is a journey of a thousand steps, and every step forward is a victory worth acknowledging.

I also want to address a topic that's often overlooked in language learning resources: the emotional aspect of this journey. Learning a new language can be an incredibly vulnerable experience. It requires us to step out of our comfort zones, to make mistakes in front of others, and sometimes to feel like we're not making progress as quickly as we'd like.

As teachers and parents, we must create an environment where it's safe to make mistakes. Where laughter is encouraged, not at the expense of others, but as a shared experience of the sometimes funny situations that arise when learning a new language. Where effort is praised just as much as results, and where every learner feels valued for their unique contributions to the classroom or family dynamic.

This emotional support is just as crucial as any teaching technique or learning strategy. It's what gives learners the courage to keep trying, to push through difficulties, and to see challenges as opportunities rather than roadblocks.

As we wrap up this introduction, I want to leave you with a thought that has guided me throughout my teaching career: language is not just a skill to be learned but a gift to be shared. Every word we teach and every conversation we have is an opportunity to build bridges between cultures, foster understanding, and empower individuals to share their unique voices with the world.

So, as we embark on this ESL journey together, let's approach it not just as teachers, parents, or students but as fellow explorers in the vast and wonderful world of language. Let's be curious, be kind to ourselves and others, and above all, let's enjoy the adventure.

Carry these reflections with you as we move forward. Let them inspire you, motivate you, and remind you of the incredible potential that lies within every language learner.

So, are you ready to embark on this exciting journey of empowering English learners? Let's turn the page together and begin our exploration of the beautiful world of ESL teaching and learning. The adventure awaits!

- Chapter 1 -

UNDERSTANDING THE BASICS OF ESL LEARNING

Defining ESL and Its Global Significance

I did not anticipate how teaching English as a Second Language (ESL) would significantly shape my perspective on language, culture, and interpersonal dynamics. ESL is about opening doors to new worlds of potential, not merely teaching vocabulary lists and grammar standards.

The study of English by non-native speakers is the fundamental definition of ESL. In my experience, however, it goes well beyond that. It serves as a cultural bridge, a means of facilitating international connection, and frequently a route to improved educational and professional opportunities.

In the business world, English proficiency can be the difference between landing that dream job or watching opportunities pass by. I've had students who were brilliant engineers or talented artists, but their lack of English skills held them back from advancing in their careers. Mastering ESL opened up new horizons for them, allowing their talents to shine on a global stage.

But ESL isn't just about career advancement. It's about cultural exchange, broadening perspectives, and fostering global understanding. I've witnessed beautiful moments in my classroom where students from different countries who couldn't communicate at the start of the term became fast friends by the end - all through the power of a shared language.

Learning English as a second language can be particularly impactful for children. In many countries, English is the language of instruction for higher education. By mastering ESL, these kids aren't just learning a new language—they're securing access to better educational opportunities down the road.

Moreover, in our digital age, English proficiency allows children to engage with a wealth of online resources, from educational videos to international pen pals. I've seen shy students blossom as they discover they can communicate with kids their age from around the world through English.

It's important to note that embracing ESL doesn't mean abandoning one's native language or culture. In fact, I always encourage my students to see their multilingual abilities as a superpower. Being able to navigate multiple languages and cultures is an incredible asset in our global society.

As we delve deeper into ESL learning strategies in this guide, it's crucial to keep this bigger picture in mind. We're not just teaching or learning a language - we're opening doors, building bridges, and empowering individuals to participate fully in our interconnected world.

Navigating ESL Challenges: A Roadmap for Parents

Learning a new language is never a smooth, straight path. It's more like a winding road with unexpected twists, steep climbs, and sometimes, moments where you feel like you're going backward. As a parent supporting an ESL learner, understanding these challenges is the first step in helping your child navigate them successfully.

One of the biggest hurdles I've observed in my years of teaching is the emotional rollercoaster that comes with language learning. There's the initial excitement of starting something new, followed by the frustration of not being able to express oneself fully. I remember a young student, Alex, who burst into tears one day because he couldn't find the words to tell me about his new puppy. It broke my heart, but it also reinforced how crucial emotional support is in this journey.

Parents, your role here is invaluable. It is crucial to create a safe, judgment-free space at home where your child feels comfortable making mistakes. Celebrate the small victories—the first time they understand an English TV show without subtitles or when they successfully order at a restaurant in English. These moments of pride can fuel motivation during the more challenging times.

Another common challenge is the fear of speaking. Many ESL learners, especially children, feel self-conscious about their accents or worry about making grammatical mistakes. This fear can lead to reluctance to practice speaking, creating a vicious cycle where lack of practice leads to slower improvement.

To combat this, try incorporating English into daily life in low-pressure ways. Have casual conversations in English during dinner or play word games as a family. The key is to make English feel like a natural part of life, not just a subject to be studied.

Inconsistent progress is another hurdle that can be particularly frustrating for both learners and parents. Language learning often follows a pattern of rapid improvement followed by plateaus, where progress seems to stall. I've had countless worried parents come to me saying, "My child was doing so well, but now they seem stuck!"

It's crucial to understand that these plateaus are a normal part of the learning process. They're often periods where the brain is consolidating knowledge, even if it's not immediately apparent. During these times, encouragement and patience are critical. Mix up learning activities to keep things fresh, but avoid putting pressure on your child to show constant, visible progress.

Cultural differences can also pose challenges in ESL learning. Language is deeply intertwined with culture, and sometimes, concepts or expressions take time to translate. I once had a student who was confused by the phrase "it's raining cats and dogs" because, in her culture, there was no equivalent idiom.

As a parent, you can turn these moments of cultural confusion into opportunities for learning and discussion. Please encourage your child to share these differences they notice and explore them together. It's a chance not just to learn English but to broaden cultural understanding.

Time management is another common struggle, especially for school-age ESL learners who are juggling language learning with their regular studies. It's easy for English practice to get pushed to the back burner when homework piles up.

Establishing a routine can be incredibly helpful here. Set aside specific times for English practice, even if it's just 15 minutes a day. Consistency is more important than duration. You might also look for ways to incorporate English into other subjects—for instance, watching science videos in English to supplement science homework.

Lastly, many ESL learners need help with the disconnect between classroom English and real-world usage. They might excel at grammar exercises but freeze up in actual conversations. This is where exposure to authentic English content becomes crucial.

Encourage your child to engage with English media - books, movies, podcasts, YouTube videos - that align with their interests. If they love soccer, they could follow English-language soccer news. If they're into cooking, try following some English recipe videos together. The goal is to make English a living language, not just a school subject.

As we navigate these challenges, it's essential to maintain a positive attitude. Every struggle is an opportunity for growth, and every mistake is a stepping stone to fluency. Your support and encouragement as a parent can make all the difference in your child's ESL journey.

Creating a Language-Rich Home Environment

When it comes to ESL learning, the classroom is just one piece of the puzzle. The home environment plays a crucial role in reinforcing and expanding on what's learned in formal lessons. As a parent, you have the power to transform your home into a rich, engaging language-learning space.

First and foremost, it's essential to fill your home with English-language resources. Books are a fantastic place to start. I always tell my students' parents: "A book is a window to a new world." Even if your child is still getting ready to read complex novels in English, picture books, comic books, or magazines can be great starting points.

I remember visiting the home of one of my young students, Yuki. Her parents had created a cozy reading nook in the corner of the living room, filled with English books at various levels. Yuki proudly showed me how she had progressed from simple picture books to chapter books over a year. The joy on her face as she read a passage from her current book was priceless.

But go beyond books. In our digital age, there's a wealth of English-language content available at our fingertips. Streaming services often offer the option to watch shows and movies in English with subtitles—a great way to improve listening skills while also supporting comprehension. Podcasts, audiobooks, and YouTube videos can also be valuable resources.

One creative idea I've seen work well is creating an "English zone" in the house. This could be a corner of a room where only English is spoken. Fill it with English books, games, and a tablet or computer to access English content. Make it a fun, inviting space that your child wants to spend time in.

Music is another powerful tool for language learning. English songs can help with pronunciation, vocabulary, and even cultural understanding. Plus, they're just plain fun! I've had students who learned more from their favorite English songs than from any textbook. Create playlists of English songs and play them during car rides or while doing chores around the house.

Speaking of chores, everyday activities provide excellent opportunities for casual English practice. Cooking together? Read the recipe in English. Doing laundry? Practice vocabulary for clothes and colors. Going grocery shopping? Make the shopping list in English and practice asking for items at the store.

Games are another fantastic way to create a language-rich environment at home. Board games, card games, and even simple word games like I Spy can all be played in English, making language practice feel like fun rather than work. One family I worked with had a weekly "English Game Night" where they'd play games and watch a movie in English - it became a cherished family tradition.

Technology can be a great ally in creating an English-rich environment. Numerous language learning apps are available that can turn a few minutes of downtime into a quick English lesson.

Just be sure to balance screen time with other forms of engagement.

One often overlooked aspect of creating a language-rich environment is the power of conversation. Make an effort to have regular conversations in English with your child. It doesn't have to be about anything complex - talk about their day, their friends, their hobbies. The goal is to get them comfortable expressing themselves in English.

If you're not confident in your English skills, don't let that hold you back. Learning alongside your child can be a bonding experience. I've seen beautiful moments where parents and children support each other, celebrate each other's progress, and laugh together at mistakes.

It's also worth considering the physical environment. Labels can be a simple yet effective tool. Put English labels on objects around the house - it's a passive way to reinforce vocabulary. You could even make it a project to create these labels together.

Inviting English into your home doesn't mean banishing your native language. The goal is to create a bilingual environment where both languages are valued and used. This not only supports English learning but also reinforces the importance of maintaining the home language.

One family I worked with had a clever system: they'd speak their native language at breakfast and dinner, but lunch was "English time." This allowed for a balance of both languages and created a designated time for English practice.

Creating a language-rich environment at home is about more than just surrounding your child with English resources. It's about fostering a positive attitude towards language learning, making it a natural, enjoyable part of daily life rather than a chore.

I always emphasize to parents that consistency is vital. It's better to have 15 minutes of English engagement every day than a three-hour cram session once a week. Make English a regular part of your family routine, and you'll be amazed at how quickly it becomes second nature.

Be patient with both yourself and your child as you set out to create a home environment that is rich in English. There will be days when you don't feel motivated or when things seem to be moving slowly. Back to the fun stuff on these days: play a game, sing some English songs, or watch your favorite English-language film. Maintaining a pleasant and good experience is the aim.

A language-rich environment is a gift you're giving your child - a gift that will open doors and create opportunities for years to come. Embrace the process, celebrate the small victories, and most importantly, have fun with it. After all, language is about connection, and there's no better place to foster that connection than at home.

- Chapter 2 -
THE ROLE OF TEACHERS IN ESL EDUCATION

The Critical Role of Teachers in ESL Education

As an ESL teacher, I've come to realize that our role extends far beyond just imparting language skills. We're not merely instructors; we're facilitators, mentors, cultural ambassadors, and sometimes even surrogate family members for our students. The impact we have on our learners' lives can be profound and long-lasting.

In my years of teaching, I've witnessed countless moments where a teacher's influence has been the catalyst for a student's breakthrough. It's not always about perfectly executed lesson plans or innovative teaching methods. Often, it's the small, human interactions that make the most significant difference - a word of encouragement when a student is struggling, a moment of shared laughter over a language mix-up, or the pride in a student's eyes when they master a difficult concept.

One of the most crucial aspects of our role is creating a safe, welcoming environment where students feel comfortable taking risks with the language. Learning a new language requires vulnerability - students must be willing to make mistakes, sound 'funny,' and express complex thoughts with limited vocabulary. As teachers, we set the tone for this. When we respond to errors with patience and encouragement rather than criticism, when we celebrate attempts as much as successes, we're fostering an atmosphere where learning can flourish.

We're also often the primary source of authentic language input for our students. In many cases, especially in EFL (English as a Foreign Language) contexts, we might be the only native or fluent English speakers our students interact with regularly. This puts us in a unique position to model natural language use, introduce cultural nuances, and provide context that textbooks alone can't offer.

Beyond language instruction, ESL teachers play a vital role in helping students navigate cultural differences. Language and culture are inextricably linked, and learning English often involves grappling with unfamiliar cultural concepts. As teachers, we serve as cultural interpreters, helping students understand not just the words but the worldview embedded in the language.

Moreover, for many ESL students, particularly young learners or recent immigrants, we're not just teaching a language - we're providing a lifeline to their new environment. I've had students confide in me about struggles with culture shock, homesickness, or difficulty making friends. In these moments, our role expands to that of a counselor and advocate.

The relationships we build with our students can have a lasting impact on their language-learning journey. When students trust and respect their teacher, they're more likely to engage fully with the learning process, take risks with the language, and persist through challenges. I've had former students reach out years later to share how our classes influenced their educational or career paths, reinforcing the long-term impact of our work.

Another critical aspect of our role is adapting our teaching to meet diverse learning needs. ESL classrooms are often highly heterogeneous, with students from various linguistic and cultural backgrounds with different levels of proficiency, learning styles, and motivations. Skillful ESL teachers must be adept at differentiation, providing multiple entry points to learning and tailoring instruction to individual needs.

We also serve as a bridge between our students and the broader educational system. For ESL students in mainstream education, we often advocate for their needs, helping other teachers understand the challenges of learning content in a second language and suggesting accommodations or modifications.

Ultimately, as ESL teachers, we're not just teaching a subject - we're empowering our students to find their voice in a new language. We're opening doors to opportunities, fostering intercultural understanding, and, sometimes, changing the trajectory of our students' lives. It's a responsibility that comes with challenges but also with immense rewards. Every time a student gains the confidence to express themselves in English, every time they achieve a goal that once seemed out of reach, we share in that triumph. That's the true power and privilege of our role as ESL teachers.

Teaching Environments and Essential Skills for ESL Educators

The landscape of ESL teaching is diverse, with each environment presenting its own unique set of challenges and opportunities. Throughout my career, I've had the chance to teach in various settings, from traditional classrooms to online platforms, and each has required a slightly different skill set. However, some core competencies are essential for all ESL teachers, regardless of the specific teaching environment.

Let's start by exploring some of the typical teaching environments in ESL education:

- **Traditional Classroom:** This is the most familiar setting for many teachers. In a conventional classroom, you're face-to-face with your students, able to pick up on non-verbal cues and create a more immersive language environment. The challenge here often lies in managing diverse proficiency levels within a single class and keeping all students engaged.

- **Language Schools:** These specialized institutions focus solely on language instruction. Classes are often intensive and may cater to specific purposes like business English or exam preparation. Teaching in this environment requires a deep understanding of language acquisition principles and the ability to tailor instruction to specific learner goals.

- **Online Teaching:** With the rise of digital technology, online ESL teaching has become increasingly popular. This virtual environment offers flexibility and a dynamic face-to-face experience, though it presents unique challenges, such as engaging students through a screen and addressing technical issues.

- **One-on-One Tutoring:** Whether in-person or online, one-on-one tutoring allows for highly personalized instruction. It requires strong interpersonal skills and the ability to assess and adapt to individual learner needs quickly.

- **Small Group Classes:** Small group classes provide a collaborative learning environment, allowing students to engage with both the instructor and their peers. This setup encourages interaction and shared learning experiences, which can boost motivation and language retention. Teaching small groups requires balancing personalized attention with group dynamics, facilitating peer-to-peer discussions, and creating activities that promote cooperative learning.

- **Corporate Training:** Teaching English in a business context often involves working with adult learners who have specific, job-related language needs. This environment requires a good understanding of business English and the ability to create practical, relevant lessons.

- **Community Programs:** These include teaching immigrants or refugees, often with limited resources. This environment requires cultural sensitivity, creativity in resource use, and, frequently, the ability to teach multi-level classes.

Now, considering these diverse environments, what skills are essential for ESL teachers? Based on my experience and conversations with colleagues, I'd highlight the following:

- **Adaptability:** This is perhaps the most crucial skill for any ESL teacher. Every class, every student, and every lesson can bring unexpected challenges. The ability to think on your feet, adjust your teaching style, and find creative solutions is invaluable.

- **Cultural Sensitivity:** ESL classrooms are often melting pots of diverse cultures. A good ESL teacher needs to be aware of and sensitive to cultural differences, able to navigate potential cultural misunderstandings, and skilled at creating an inclusive classroom environment.

- **Strong Communication Skills:** This goes beyond just being fluent in English. ESL teachers need to be able to explain complex language concepts in simple terms, give clear instructions, and communicate effectively with students of varying proficiency levels.

- **Patience and Empathy:** Learning a new language can be frustrating and intimidating. ESL teachers need to be patient and allow students to progress at their own pace, as well as empathic to understand and address the emotional aspects of language learning.

- **Technological Proficiency:** In today's digital age, even traditional classroom teachers need to be comfortable with technology. This might involve using language learning apps, creating digital materials, or navigating online teaching platforms.

- **Creativity:** ESL teachers often need to find innovative ways to explain concepts, design engaging activities, and make the most of limited resources. Creativity in lesson planning and delivery can make a massive difference in student engagement and learning outcomes.

- **Strong Classroom Management Skills:** This is particularly important in group settings. ESL teachers need to be able to manage different personalities, maintain discipline, and create a positive learning environment.

- **Knowledge of Language Acquisition Theories:** Understanding how people learn languages can inform teaching strategies and help teachers set realistic expectations for student progress. Total Physical Response (TPR) is an effective language teaching approach that combines language with physical movement to enhance comprehension and retention. By using hand gestures, body language, and actions to convey meaning, teachers help students associate words and phrases with physical responses. This method is especially useful for younger learners and beginners, as it makes learning interactive and engaging. Incorporating TPR can build student confidence, make new vocabulary more memorable, and create a fun, immersive learning experience that aids in long-term language retention.

- **Flexibility:** ESL teaching often involves working with diverse age groups, proficiency levels, and learning styles—sometimes all within the same class. The ability to adapt your teaching style to meet diverse needs is crucial.

- **Continuous Learning Mindset:** The field of ESL is constantly evolving, with new methodologies, technologies, and best practices emerging. Successful ESL teachers embrace lifelong learning and continuously seek to improve their skills and knowledge.

- **Assessment Skills:** Accurately assessing student progress and providing constructive feedback is a vital part of the ESL teacher's role. This involves both formal assessment methods and the ability to gauge student understanding in day-to-day interactions.

- **Lesson Planning and Curriculum Development:** While many teaching environments provide a curriculum, the ability to plan practical lessons and even develop curriculum materials is a valuable skill for ESL teachers.

These skills form the foundation of effective ESL teaching across various environments. However, it's important to note that developing these skills is an ongoing process. Even after years of teaching, I find myself constantly learning, adapting, and refining my approach.

The beauty of ESL teaching lies in its dynamic nature. Every class, every student brings new challenges and opportunities for growth. By continuously honing these essential skills and remaining open to new experiences, we can not only become more effective teachers but also find greater fulfillment in our roles as educators and cultural bridges.

Effective Communication Strategies between Teachers, Parents, and Students

In the world of ESL education, effective communication is the glue that holds everything together. It's the conduit through which understanding flows, progress is tracked, and support is provided. Throughout my teaching career, I've come to appreciate that successful language learning is truly a collaborative effort between teachers, parents, and students. When this triad of stakeholders communicates effectively, the benefits to the learner are immense.

First and foremost, it's crucial to establish open lines of communication from the very beginning. As a teacher, I make it a point to reach out to parents early in the school year or course duration. This initial contact sets the tone for ongoing communication and demonstrates that I value parental involvement in their child's language learning journey.

One strategy I've found particularly effective is offering a trial class where we meet with students and parents to introduce them to the program. This session, based on the student's placement test results, provides an opportunity to discuss goals and expectations, and it can take place at any time throughout the year, as enrollment is open on a rolling basis. This can be done in person or virtually, depending on the teaching context. During this session, I outline my teaching approach, expectations for the course, and, importantly, how I plan to communicate with parents throughout the year. I also use this opportunity to learn about parents' preferred communication methods—whether that's email, messaging apps like WhatsApp or WeChat, or phone calls—to effectively gather details about the learner's goals and needs, especially when in-person meetings aren't possible.

Regular updates are vital in maintaining good communication. However, the frequency and format of these updates can vary depending on the teaching context and the needs of the students and parents. In some cases, weekly progress reports might be appropriate, while in others, monthly updates might suffice. Additionally, providing immediate class feedback after each lesson, accessible through a student account, can keep parents and students consistently informed on progress and areas for growth. The key is consistency and relevance - parents should know when to expect updates and what kind of information they'll receive.

These updates should focus on more than academic progress. I share positive observations about a student's efforts, improvements in confidence, or instances where they've shown particular enthusiasm. This holistic approach gives parents a more complete picture of their child's language learning journey.

Of course, communication isn't just about the teacher sharing information - it's a two-way street. I always encourage parents to reach out with any concerns, questions, or insights about their child's learning. Sometimes, parents might notice struggles or breakthroughs at home that aren't apparent in the classroom. This information can be invaluable in tailoring instruction to meet a student's needs.

Clarity and consistency are paramount when communicating with students. Establishing clear expectations and routines from the outset helps students feel secure in the learning environment. This might involve creating a visual schedule for younger learners or providing a detailed syllabus for older students.

I'm also a big believer in the power of positive reinforcement in communication with students. Celebrating small victories, acknowledging effort, and providing specific, constructive feedback can go a long way in building a student's confidence and motivation.

Fostering a sense of ownership over one's learning can be incredibly empowering for older students. I often involve students in setting their own language learning goals and regularly check in on their progress. This not only improves communication but also helps students develop valuable self-reflection and goal-setting skills.

In today's digital age, technology can be a powerful tool for enhancing communication between teachers, parents, and students. Learning management systems, for instance, can provide a centralized platform for sharing resources, tracking progress, and facilitating discussions. However, it's crucial to ensure that the use of technology doesn't create barriers for those who have limited access or technical skills.

One communication strategy that I've found particularly effective is student-led conferences. In these sessions, students take the lead in discussing their progress with their parents, with the teacher acting as a facilitator. This approach not only improves communication but also helps students develop essential skills in self-assessment and articulation of their learning.

Cultural sensitivity is another crucial aspect of effective communication in ESL contexts. It's essential to be aware that communication norms can vary significantly across cultures. Some parents might be accustomed to a more formal communication style with teachers, while others might expect more frequent, casual interactions. Being flexible and responsive to these cultural differences can go a long way in building solid and positive relationships with families.

When challenges or concerns arise, addressing them promptly and constructively is vital. I always strive to approach these conversations with a problem-solving mindset, focusing on collaborative solutions rather than assigning blame. It's also essential to maintain student confidentiality in these discussions, especially when communicating with parents of adult learners.

One of the most powerful communication tools is simply being approachable and available. Whether it's staying a few minutes after class to chat with students, holding regular office hours, or being responsive to parent emails, showing that you're accessible and willing to listen can foster a sense of trust and partnership that enhances the entire learning experience.

Effective communication in ESL education is an ongoing process of listening, sharing, and adapting. When teachers, parents, and students are all on the same page, working together towards shared goals, the potential for language learning success is limitless. It's not always easy, and it certainly requires effort and dedication from all parties involved. But in my experience, the rewards - in terms of student progress, parent satisfaction, and overall teaching effectiveness - are well worth the investment.

Supporting Language Development Outside the Classroom

As ESL teachers, our influence extends far beyond the confines of the classroom. We have the unique opportunity - and, I'd argue, the responsibility - to empower our students and their families to continue the language learning journey outside of formal instruction time. After all, language acquisition is not confined to the hours spent in a classroom; it's a continuous process that can be integrated into everyday life.

One of the most impactful ways we can support language development outside the classroom is by helping parents create a language-rich environment at home. This doesn't mean turning every moment into a formal English lesson but instead finding natural, enjoyable ways to incorporate English into daily routines.

I often suggest to parents that they designate certain activities or times of day as 'English time.' This could be as simple as having English-language music playing during breakfast or reading an

English bedtime story. The key is consistency and making it a positive, stress-free experience.

Another excellent way is to involve them in watching English media with the parents. That way, you can watch English-speaking TV or films together, with or without subtitles, depending on your needs, for making topics of conversation and bringing in new vocabulary in context. I often make suggestions to parents regarding a list of age-appropriate shows, YouTube channels, or podcasts that appeal to the interests of their child and match his language level.

For families where the parents need more confidence in their own English speakers, I emphasize that perfect fluency isn't necessary to support their child's learning. Even simple activities like learning and using a new English word together each day can make a difference. It's about creating a positive attitude towards English and showing that language learning is a lifelong journey.

Another effective strategy is providing 'home learning kits' that families can use together. These might include themed flashcard sets on topics like phonics, animals, and time, as well as simple board games, conversation starter cards, or scavenger hunt lists. These materials encourage students to practice English in engaging, interactive ways at home. These include simple board games that practice specific language skills, conversation starter cards, or scavenger hunt lists that encourage students to find and describe objects around their home in English.

Technology can be a powerful ally in supporting out-of-class learning. Numerous language learning apps and websites can make practice feel more like play. However, I always stress to parents the importance of balancing screen time with other forms of engagement. A mix of digital and non-digital activities is most effective.

Encouraging real-world language use is another crucial aspect of supporting out-of-class learning. This might involve suggesting that older students order for themselves in English at restaurants or encouraging families to visit local tourist spots and practice describing what they see in English. These authentic language experiences can be incredibly motivating and help students see the practical value of their English skills.

For students from immigrant communities, I often recommend getting involved in community events or programs where they can use English in a supportive environment. This might include joining sports teams, attending library story times, or participating in community service activities. These experiences not only provide language practice but also help students feel more connected to their new community.

Writing can sometimes be overlooked in out-of-class language support, but it's a crucial skill to develop. I often suggest fun writing activities that families can do together, like keeping a shared English journal, writing and illustrating short stories, or even starting a family blog about their ESL journey.

For older students or adults, I emphasize the importance of finding ways to integrate English into their personal interests or career goals. This might involve reading English-language articles or books related to their field, joining online forums or social media groups centered around their hobbies, or seeking out English-language networking opportunities in their industry.

One strategy that I've found particularly effective is encouraging students to become 'teachers' themselves. When students explain English concepts to siblings or parents, it not only reinforces their learning but also boosts their confidence. I often provide simple lesson ideas or conversation prompts that students can use to 'teach' their families.

Creating a support network can also be invaluable for out-of-class learning. I connect families with similar language backgrounds or learning goals, encouraging them to organize playdates, study groups, or language exchange sessions. This peer support can be incredibly motivating and provide additional opportunities for authentic language use.

It's important to note that supporting out-of-class learning isn't about adding pressure or turning every moment into a lesson. It's about creating an environment where English feels accessible, enjoyable, and relevant to everyday life. I always emphasize to parents and students that consistency is more important than intensity - small, regular engagements with English will yield better results than occasional cram sessions.

- Chapter 3 -
THE ROLE OF PARENTS IN ESL EDUCATION

The Critical Role of Parents in Their Child's ESL Education

As an ESL educator, I've come to realize that our student's parents are our most powerful allies in their language-learning journey. Parents' influence on a child's educational success cannot be overstated, and this is particularly true when it comes to learning English as a second language.

Parents are their children's first teachers, and this role remains the same when formal education begins. In fact, parental involvement becomes even more crucial when a child is navigating the challenges of learning a new language. The home environment, family attitudes toward learning English, and the support provided outside the classroom all play pivotal roles in a child's ESL success.

One of the most significant ways parents impact their child's ESL education is through their attitude toward language learning. When parents demonstrate enthusiasm for English and show that they value bilingualism, children are more likely to approach their ESL studies with positivity and motivation. This positive attitude can be the difference between a child seeing English as a chore and viewing it as an exciting opportunity.

Moreover, parents have the unique ability to provide context and relevance to their child's English learning. They can help bridge the gap between what's learned in the classroom and how it applies to real life. When parents show interest in what their child is learning and find ways to incorporate it into daily life, it reinforces the importance and practicality of English skills.

Another critical aspect of parental involvement is the emotional support they provide. Learning a new language can be frustrating and sometimes overwhelming for children. Parents are in the best position to offer encouragement, celebrate small victories, and provide a safe space for their children to practice without fear of judgment. This emotional scaffolding is invaluable in building a child's confidence and resilience in their language learning journey.

Parents also play a crucial role in maintaining and developing their child's first language. Research has shown that a strong foundation in one's native language actually supports the acquisition of a second language. By encouraging the use of the home language alongside English, parents can foster true bilingualism, which has numerous cognitive and cultural benefits.

Furthermore, parents are often the ones who can provide the most consistent exposure to English outside of school hours. Whether it's through English media, books, or simply conversing in English at home, this additional exposure can significantly accelerate a child's language acquisition. Parents have the power to turn everyday moments into language learning opportunities, reinforcing what's been taught in the classroom and providing real-world context for language use.

It's also worth noting that parents serve as critical cultural mediators for their ESL children. They can help their children navigate the artistic aspects of language learning, explaining idioms, customs, or social norms that might be confusing. This cultural context is often as important as the language itself in achieving true fluency.

Additionally, parents are crucial advocates for their children in the educational system. They can communicate with teachers about their child's needs, challenges, and progress, ensuring that their child receives appropriate support and resources. This advocacy role is vital for ESL students who may face unique challenges in the mainstream education system.

However, it's essential to acknowledge that supporting a child's ESL education can be challenging for many parents, especially if they need more confidence in their own English speakers. As educators, we need to be sensitive to this and provide support and resources to help parents feel empowered in this role.

Even parents who don't speak English fluently can have a tremendous positive impact on their child's language learning. It's not about being a perfect English speaker but about showing interest, providing opportunities for practice, and maintaining a positive attitude towards language learning. It's about being "present" in this learning journey with your children.

The involvement of parents in ESL education also extends to cultural preservation. While learning English is essential, it shouldn't come at the cost of losing connection to one's heritage language and culture. Parents play a vital role in helping their children balance both worlds, fostering an additive bilingualism where English is learned in addition to, not instead of, the home language.

Ultimately, parents' role in ESL education is multifaceted and profound. They are motivators, facilitators, advocates, and co-learners in their child's language journey. When parents are actively engaged in their child's ESL education, it sends a powerful message about the value of language learning and sets the stage for long-term success.

As educators, recognizing and supporting this parental role is crucial. By fostering strong partnerships with parents, we can create a more holistic and practical ESL learning experience for our students. The synergy between classroom instruction and home support can lead to remarkable progress in a child's English proficiency and overall academic success.

Effective Communication Strategies Between Teachers, Parents, and Students

In my years as an ESL educator, I've come to understand that effective communication is the cornerstone of successful language learning. When teachers, parents, and students are all on the same page, working together towards shared goals, the potential for progress is limitless. However, achieving this level of communication can be challenging, especially when language barriers and cultural differences come into play.

The first step in establishing effective communication is to create an open and welcoming environment. As teachers, we need to make it clear from the outset that we value parental involvement and see parents as partners in their child's education. This might involve offering a virtual orientation session upon enrollment, where parents can meet teachers, learn about the ESL program, and ask questions in a relaxed online setting. This approach allows families to connect with the school community and gain insights into the program at their convenience.

It's crucial to recognize that communication preferences can vary widely among families. Some parents prefer face-to-face meetings, while others might find email or messaging apps more convenient. As educators, we need to be flexible and willing to adapt our communication methods to meet the needs of each family. Asking parents about their preferred mode of communication early on can prevent misunderstandings and ensure that critical information doesn't fall through the cracks.

Regular updates are vital to maintaining good communication. However, these updates should go beyond just reporting grades or behavioral issues. Parents want to know about their child's progress, but they also want to hear about their strengths, challenges, and how they can support learning at home. I make it a point to share positive observations and small victories, not just areas for improvement. This balanced approach helps build a more positive and collaborative relationship with parents.

Language barriers can often be a significant obstacle to effective communication with ESL families. As teachers, we need to be proactive in addressing this challenge. This might involve providing translated materials, using simple language in our communications, or enlisting the help of interpreters for parent-teacher conferences. Even small efforts, like learning a few key phrases in a family's home language, can go a long way in building trust and showing respect for their cultural background.

Another effective strategy is to involve students in the communication process. Student-led conferences, where children take the lead in discussing their progress with their parents and teachers, can be compelling. This approach improves communication and helps students develop essential skills in self-reflection and goal-setting.

Technology can be a valuable tool in facilitating communication between teachers, parents, and students. Learning management systems, class websites, or even simple messaging apps can provide platforms for sharing resources, updating class activities, and facilitating ongoing dialogue. However, it's essential to ensure that the use of technology doesn't create barriers for families with limited access to digital literacy skills.

One communication strategy that I've found particularly effective is the use of 'communication journals' or 'dialogue books.' These notebooks travel between home and school, where teachers, parents, and students can share observations, ask questions, or provide updates. This ongoing dialogue helps create a sense of continuity between home and school learning.

It's also essential to create opportunities for informal communication. While formal parent-teacher conferences are important, sometimes the most valuable exchanges happen in more relaxed settings. This might involve staying a few minutes after class to chat with parents during pick-up time or organizing casual coffee mornings where parents can connect with teachers and each other.

Cultural sensitivity is crucial in communication with ESL families. It's essential to be aware that communication norms can vary significantly across cultures. Some cultures, for example, may view direct questioning of a teacher as disrespectful, while others may expect more frequent communication than is typical in the local school system. Being aware of and responsive to these cultural differences can help prevent misunderstandings and build stronger relationships with families.

When challenges or concerns arise, addressing them promptly and constructively is critical. I always strive to approach these conversations with a problem-solving mindset, focusing on collaborative solutions rather than assigning blame. It's also essential to maintain student confidentiality in these discussions, especially when communicating with parents of adult learners.

Another critical aspect of effective communication is active listening. As teachers, we need to create spaces where parents feel heard and valued. This might involve setting aside time for parent feedback sessions or simply being attentive and responsive when parents share concerns or insights about their child's learning.

Empowering parents to be advocates for their children is also a crucial part of effective communication. This might involve providing information about the school system, explaining educational jargon, or guiding parents on how to effectively communicate their concerns or questions to other educators or administrators.

Lastly, it's essential to recognize and celebrate the diverse strengths that ESL families bring to the school community. Creating opportunities for parents to share their cultural knowledge, skills, or experiences can enrich the learning environment for all students and foster a more inclusive school community.

Effective communication in ESL education is an ongoing process that requires effort, patience, and flexibility from all parties involved. However, when we get it right, the benefits are immense. Strong communication channels between teachers, parents, and students create a supportive ecosystem where language learning can thrive, both in and out of the classroom.

Ways Parents Can Actively Support Their Child's Language Development Outside the Classroom

As an ESL educator, one of the most frequent questions I receive from parents is, "How can I help my child learn English at home?" The truth is that the support that parents provide outside the classroom can be just as crucial as formal instruction in a child's language development. The home environment offers countless opportunities for natural, contextual language learning that can significantly boost a child's English skills.

First and foremost, parents can create an English-rich environment at home. This doesn't mean banishing the home language—bilingualism is a strength to be nurtured. Instead, it's about incorporating English into daily life in natural, enjoyable ways. This might involve designating certain times of day as 'English time,' when the family tries to communicate primarily in English. For example, dinner time could become an opportunity for English conversation practice.

Reading together in English is one of the most powerful ways parents can support their child's language development. Even if parents need more confidence in their own English skills, simply sitting together and looking at English books can be beneficial. Picture books, comics, or age-appropriate magazines can be great starting points. As children progress, parents can encourage them to read aloud, discuss the story, and explain unfamiliar words.

Engaging with English media together is another effective strategy. Watching English-language TV shows, movies, or YouTube videos with subtitles can introduce new vocabulary and improve listening skills. I suggest that families have discussions about what they've watched, encouraging children to express their thoughts in English. This not only reinforces language skills but also critical thinking and comprehension.

Music is a powerful tool for language learning that parents can easily incorporate into daily life. Listening to English songs, learning lyrics together, or even having family karaoke nights can make language practice fun and memorable. Music can help with pronunciation, vocabulary, and even cultural understanding.

Games are another enjoyable way to practice English at home. Board games, card games, or even simple word games like I Spy can provide opportunities for language use in a low-pressure, fun environment. Parents can also create their games, like scavenger hunts around the house, where children have to find and describe objects in English. You can even use flashcards for games.

Flashcard Games

Card Slap: Scatter cards at random across a surface. When you say a letter (or word), the child will slap the card with their hand.

Order Up: Scatter cards and have the child place them in alphabetical order.

Mums the Word: Without using your voice, mouth the letter (or word) and have child point to the correct card and say it out loud.

Cover Up: Cover the picture and have the child think of (or draw) words that begin with the letter.

For families where parents are learners themselves, learning English together can be a powerful bonding experience. This might involve taking an online course together, practicing with language learning apps, or simply learning and using a new English word or phrase each day as a family.

Another effective strategy is to incorporate English into everyday activities. This might involve cooking together using English recipes, making shopping lists in English, or describing daily routines in English. These practical applications help children see the relevance of their language learning to real life.

Encouraging children to keep an English journal or diary can support both writing skills and self-expression. Parents can provide prompts or topics if needed and make it a regular family activity to share what they've written.

For older children or teens, parents can encourage engagement with English through their interests or hobbies. This might involve finding English-language blogs, podcasts, or YouTube channels related to their passions. When language learning aligns with personal interests, motivation and retention tend to increase.

Creating opportunities for authentic language use is crucial. This might involve encouraging children to order for themselves in English at restaurants, interact with English-speaking tourists in your area, or participate in community events where English is used. These real-world experiences can be incredibly motivating and confidence-building.

Technology can be a valuable ally in at-home language learning. Numerous apps and websites designed for English learners can make practice feel more like play. However, it's important to balance screen time with other forms of engagement and ensure that digital tools supplement human interaction.

Parents can also support language development by helping their children set language learning goals and tracking progress. This might involve creating a chart to track new vocabulary learned each week or setting challenges like reading a certain number of English books per month. Celebrating these achievements, no matter how small can boost motivation and confidence.

Another effective strategy is to create an 'English corner' in the home - a designated space filled with English books, games, and learning materials. This physical reminder can make English learning a natural part of daily life.

For families living in non-English speaking countries, seeking out English language events or meetups in your area can provide valuable opportunities for practice and cultural exchange. This might include attending English storytimes at local libraries, joining international clubs, or participating in language exchange programs.

Parents need to model a positive attitude towards language learning. Even if they're not confident, English speakers themselves, showing enthusiasm for learning and willingness to make mistakes, can encourage children to adopt a similar mindset.

It is crucial to maintain open communication with the child's ESL teacher. Parents should feel comfortable asking for guidance on how to support learning at home and sharing observations about their child's progress or challenges.

Supporting a child's ESL learning at home doesn't require parents to be English experts. It's about creating a supportive environment, providing opportunities for practice, and maintaining a positive attitude towards language learning. Every small effort contributes to a child's language development, and the consistent support of parents can make a world of difference in a child's ESL journey.

- Chapter 4 -

BUILDING A STRONG FOUNDATION IN ENGLISH LANGUAGE

Key Aspects of English Language Learning

Through time, as an ESL educator, I have grown to really appreciate that language learning is like building a house: if the foundation is no good, everything else falls. This foundation, in English and most of the other languages, involves four pillars holding it up, namely vocabulary, grammar, pronunciation, and writing. Each one of these facets stands by itself and interrelates with the others in developing the overall language ability.

Vocabulary is often considered the building blocks of language. Without words, we can't express our thoughts or understand others. But vocabulary isn't just about memorizing lists of words. It's about understanding how words relate to each other, how they change in different contexts, and how to use them effectively. A rich vocabulary allows learners to express themselves more precisely and understand more complex ideas.

Grammar, on the other hand, is the framework that holds these building blocks together. It's the set of rules that govern how we structure sentences and convey meaning. While some learners might find grammar daunting, understanding grammar can actually be empowering. It gives learners the tools to construct their sentences and express their unique thoughts rather than relying on memorized phrases.

Pronunciation is the most immediately noticeable aspect of language learning. It's not just about sounding "native-like" but about being understood and feeling confident in one's ability to communicate. Good pronunciation can boost a learner's confidence and make communication smoother, while poor pronunciation can lead to misunderstandings and frustration.

Writing often gets less attention in conversational English classes, but it's a crucial skill in academic and professional contexts. Writing helps consolidate grammar and vocabulary knowledge, and it allows learners to express more complex ideas than they might be able to in spontaneous speech. Moreover, in our digital age, written communication skills are more critical than ever.

These four aspects of language learning are deeply interconnected. For example, a strong vocabulary supports better writing, while understanding grammar rules can aid in pronunciation. As we explore strategies for improving each of these areas, it's essential to keep in mind how they work together to create a well-rounded language skill set.

Classroom Activities and Resources for Teachers

As teachers, our goal is to create engaging, practical lessons that address all aspects of language learning. Here are some useful activities and resources I've found helpful for each area:

1. **Vocabulary**

   - **Word Webs:** This is a great visual activity for exploring word relationships. Start with a central word and have students brainstorm related words, creating a web-like diagram. This helps students understand word families and associations.

   - **Vocabulary Journals:** Encourage students to keep a personal vocabulary journal where they record new words, their definitions, example sentences, and even drawings or associations that help them remember the word.

   - **Word of the Day:** Introduce a new word each day and challenge students to use it in conversation or writing throughout the day. This can be turned into a game, with points awarded for creative or frequent use.

2. **Grammar**

   - **Grammar Auctions:** Write sentences on strips of paper, some correct and some with errors. Students work in teams to "bid" on the sentences they believe are accurate. It's a fun way to practice identifying and correcting grammar mistakes.

- **Story Chain:** Start a story with a sentence that uses a particular grammar structure. Each student adds a sentence, continuing the story while using the same structure. This reinforces grammar rules in a creative context.

- **Grammar Board Games:** Create board games where players must correctly use specific grammar structures to advance. This turns grammar practice into a fun, competitive activity.

3. **Pronunciation**

    - **Minimal Pairs Practice:** Use pairs of words that differ by only one sound (like "sheep" and "ship") to help students distinguish between similar sounds in English.

Tongue Twisters can be frustrating but fun ways to practice specific sounds. Start with easier twisters and progress to more challenging twisters as students improve.

- **Rhythm and Stress Activities:** Use music or poetry to help students understand the rhythm and stress patterns of English. Clapping or tapping out syllables can be particularly helpful.

4. **Writing**

    - **Collaborative Writing:** Have students collaborate to write a story, with each contributing a sentence or paragraph. This can be done on paper and passed around the class or by using online tools for real-time collaboration.

- **Writing Prompts Jar:** Fill a jar with various writing prompts. Students can draw a prompt at the beginning of class for a quick writing exercise or take one home for longer writing assignments.

- **Peer Editing Workshops:** Teach students how to critique each other's writing constructively. This will improve their writing, critical thinking, and diplomacy skills.

5. Resources

Online platforms like Quizlet or Kahoot can be great for vocabulary and grammar practice.

The British Council and BBC Learning English websites offer a wealth of resources for all aspects of English learning.

TED Talks can be excellent for listening practice and writing prompts for more advanced learners.

Graphic organizers can be valuable tools for vocabulary development and writing organization.

The most effective activities are often those that integrate multiple language skills. For example, a debate activity can practice speaking, listening, and critical thinking skills while also reinforcing vocabulary and grammar.

At-Home Activities and Resources for Parents

Parents play a crucial role in supporting their child's language learning journey. Here are some practical activities and resources that parents can use at home to reinforce each aspect of English learning:

1. **Vocabulary**

    - **Word of the Day Calendar:** Create a family calendar where you introduce a new English word each day. Encourage everyone to use the word in conversation throughout the day.

    - **Vocabulary Scavenger Hunt:** Make a list of words and have your child find objects around the house that represent those words. This is particularly effective for younger learners.

    - **Crossword Puzzles:** Age-appropriate crossword puzzles can be a fun way to expand vocabulary. You can even create custom puzzles using online tools.

2. **Grammar**

    - **Grammar Game Night:** Adapt board games to include grammar challenges. For example, in Monopoly, players could be required to create a sentence using a specific grammar structure before buying a property.

    - **Sentence Building Magnets:** Use magnetic words on the refrigerator to practice building grammatically correct sentences.

- **Error Correction Challenge:** Intentionally make grammar mistakes when speaking and see if your child can spot and correct them. This can be turned into a fun family game.

3. Pronunciation

    - **Karaoke Nights:** Singing English songs can improve pronunciation and intonation in a fun, relaxed setting.

    - **Mirror Practice:** Encourage your child to practice pronouncing difficult words in front of a mirror. This visual feedback can be constructive.

    - **Pronunciation Apps:** Several apps, such as ELSA Speak or Google's Pronunciation Practice, provide pronunciation feedback.

4. Writing

    - **Family Blog or Journal:** Start a family blog or journal where everyone contributes entries about their day or thoughts on various topics.

    - **Story Dice:** Use dice with pictures or words on them to spark creative writing sessions. Roll the dice and create a story using the images or words that come up.

    - **Letter Writing:** Encourage your child to write letters to friends, family members, or even their favorite authors or characters. This practices writing in a real-world context.

5. Resources:

Websites like Duolingo or BBC Learning English offer free language learning resources that can be used at home.

English language books, comics, or magazines appropriate to your child's level can be great for vocabulary and reading practice.

Educational YouTube channels like Crash Course Kids or TED-Ed can provide engaging content for learning English.

Podcasts designed for English learners, such as "6 Minute English" from the BBC, can be great for listening practice.

The key to successful at-home learning is consistency and enjoyment. Try to incorporate English practice into daily routines in a way that feels natural and fun rather than like a chore.

Common ESL Mistakes and Teacher Strategies

In my experience, inevitable mistakes crop up repeatedly among ESL learners. Recognizing these common pitfalls can help us as teachers to address them more effectively. Here are some frequent mistakes I've encountered and strategies to help overcome them:

- **Article Usage:** Many languages need articles (a, an, the), making this a common struggle for ESL learners.
- **Strategy:** Use visual aids to demonstrate when to use each article. Practice with fill-in-the-blank exercises and encourage students to explain their choices.

- **Subject-Verb Agreement:** This can be particularly challenging for students whose native language doesn't conjugate verbs in the same way.

- **Strategy:** Use color coding to match subjects with verbs. Create games where students have to match subjects with the correct verb form quickly.

- **Prepositions:** The correct use of prepositions often only translates directly from one language to another.

- **Strategy:** Use physical demonstrations or pictures to show the relationships prepositions describe. Please encourage students to create their visual representations of prepositional phrases.

- **False Cognates:** Words that sound similar in English and the student's native language but have different meanings can confuse.

- **Strategy:** Create a "false friends" wall in the classroom where these tricky word pairs are displayed. Please encourage students to add to it as they discover new ones.

- **Pronunciation of Specific Sounds:** Certain English sounds may not exist in a student's native language, making them challenging to produce.

- **Strategy:** Use mouth diagrams to show tongue and lip positions. Practice with tongue twisters and minimal pairs focused on the problematic sounds.

- **Word Order:** The syntax of English can be very different from other languages.

- **Strategy:** Use sentence scrambles in which students must put words in the correct order. Visual aids like color-coded word cards can help reinforce correct sentence structure.

- **Irregular Verbs:** The unpredictable nature of irregular verbs in English can be frustrating for learners.

- **Strategy:** Instead of rote memorization, try grouping irregular verbs by similar patterns. Use songs or rhymes to help remember the most common ones.

- **Countable vs. Uncountable Nouns:** This distinction only exists in some languages and can be confusing for ESL learners.

- **Strategy:** Use natural objects or pictures to demonstrate the difference. Practice with sorting activities and creating shopping lists.

- **Phrasal Verbs:** These verb-preposition combinations can be particularly challenging as their meanings often can't be deduced from their parts.

- **Strategy:** Teach phrasal verbs in context through stories or role-play situations. Encourage students to keep a phrasal verb journal where they record new ones they encounter.

- **Tense Confusion:** The nuances between different English tenses, particularly in the past, can be complex for learners to grasp.

- **Strategy:** Use timelines to represent different tenses visually. Practice storytelling activities that require the use of multiple tenses.

As teachers, our role is not just to correct these mistakes but to help students understand why they're making them and how to avoid them in the future. Patience, consistent practice, and positive reinforcement are key. It's also essential to create an atmosphere where students feel comfortable making mistakes, as this is a crucial part of the learning process.

Common ESL Mistakes and Parent Strategies

Parents can play a crucial role in helping their children overcome common ESL mistakes. Here are some strategies parents can use at home:

- **Article Usage:**

Strategy: Play "I Spy" games, focusing on using articles correctly. "I spy a book" or "I spy the red car."

- **Subject-Verb Agreement:**

Strategy: Practice with simple daily reporting. At dinner, please have your child talk about their day using whole sentences, paying attention to subject-verb agreement.

- **Prepositions:**

Strategy: Use everyday objects to practice prepositions. Ask your child to place a toy "on" the table, "under" the chair, etc.

- **False Cognates:**

Strategy: Create a family "false friends" list. Whenever you or your child discovers a false cognate, add it to the list and review it together regularly.

- **Pronunciation:**

Strategy: Read aloud together, focusing on problematic sounds. Exaggerate the mouth movements for complex sounds to help your child see how they're formed.

- **Word Order:**

Strategy: Play sentence-building games. Write different words on cards and have your child arrange them to make correct sentences.

- **Irregular Verbs:**

Strategy: Create verb charts together and post them around the house. Review them casually during daily activities.

- **Countable vs. Uncountable Nouns:**

Strategy: During grocery shopping or meal preparation, practice using "much" and "many" correctly with different food items.

- **Phrasal Verbs:**

Strategy: Incorporate phrasal verbs into daily routines. For example, use "wake up," "turn off," and "put away" consistently and encourage your child to do the same.

- **Tense Confusion:**

Strategy: Practice storytelling together, using different tenses. Start a story in the present and have your child continue it in the past, or vice versa.

The key for parents is to create a supportive, low-pressure environment for language practice. Celebrate progress and treat mistakes as learning opportunities rather than failures. Remember, consistency is more important than perfection. Regular, short periods of English practice integrated into daily life can be more effective than long, infrequent study sessions.

As both teachers and parents, our goal should be to foster a love for language learning. By approaching these common challenges with patience, creativity, and positivity, we can help ESL learners build a strong foundation in English, setting them up for long-term success in their language journey.

- Chapter 5 -
TAILORING LEARNING STRATEGIES TO YOUR STUDENT'S OR CHILD'S NEEDS

The journey of learning English is as unique as the individuals embarking upon it. In my years of experience, I've witnessed the transformative power of personalized learning strategies. When we take the time to understand and cater to each learner's specific needs, we unlock their full potential and ignite a genuine passion for language acquisition.

The Importance of Understanding Learning Styles and Preferences

- **From a Teacher's Perspective:**

In the classroom, I've observed that students who struggle with traditional teaching methods often flourish when presented with approaches that align with their learning preferences. It's like finding the correct key for a lock - suddenly, everything clicks into place.

Understanding a student's learning style isn't just about making lessons more enjoyable; it's about maximizing the efficiency and effectiveness of our teaching. When we tap into a student's natural learning inclinations, we're not working against the grain but with it. This alignment can lead to faster progress, improved retention, and a boost in confidence that ripples through all aspects of their language learning journey.

Moreover, acknowledging and valuing different learning styles sends a powerful message to our students. It tells them that we see them as individuals, that we respect their unique ways of processing information, and that we're committed to their success. This recognition can be incredibly empowering for ESL students who may already feel like outsiders due to language barriers.

In my classroom, I've noticed that students become more engaged and take more ownership of their learning when they understand their learning style. It's like giving them a map to navigate their educational journey. They become more self-aware, more likely to advocate for their needs, and more adept at developing their study strategies.

However, it's crucial to note that learning styles aren't rigid categories. Students often benefit from a mix of approaches, and their preferences may evolve. Our role as teachers is to provide a diverse range of learning experiences that cater to different styles while also gently encouraging students to step out of their comfort zones and develop versatility in their learning approaches.

- **From a Parent's Perspective:**

As a parent supporting an ESL learner, understanding your child's learning style can be a game-changer. It's like having a secret decoder ring for your child's educational needs. When you know how your child best processes and retains information, you can create a home environment that supports and reinforces their classroom learning in the most effective way possible.

Recognizing your child's learning preferences can also help you advocate for them more effectively in school settings. You can communicate with teachers about what works best for your child and ensure that their unique needs are being met in the classroom.

Furthermore, this understanding can transform potentially frustrating homework sessions into productive learning experiences. By presenting information in a way that resonates with your child's learning style, you can make English practice at home more engaging and less of a chore.

It's important to remember that your child's learning style may differ from your own. What worked for you as a language learner may not be the best approach for your child. By being open to different learning strategies, you're modeling flexibility and a growth mindset - valuable skills for any language learner.

Identifying Strengths and Weaknesses in English Language Learning

- **From a Teacher's Perspective:**

Identifying a student's strengths and weaknesses in English is like creating a roadmap for their language learning journey. It helps us understand where they're starting from, what route might be best for them, and what obstacles we might encounter along the way.

In my classroom, I use a variety of assessment tools to gauge students' abilities across different language skills. This might include standardized tests, but I find that ongoing, informal assessments often provide the most valuable insights. Things like class discussions, writing assignments, listening comprehension exercises, and speaking tasks all offer windows into a student's strengths and areas for improvement.

One technique I've found particularly effective is the use of learning portfolios. These collections of a student's work over time provide a comprehensive view of their progress and help identify patterns in their learning. They also give students ownership over their learning process and a tangible way to see their improvement.

I also pay close attention to how students approach different tasks. Do they dive right into speaking activities but need help with writing assignments? Are they quick to understand grammar rules but need help with pronunciation? These observations can reveal a lot about where a student's strengths and weaknesses lie.

It's crucial to involve students in this identification process. I often have students reflect on their learning, asking them what they find easy or challenging about English. This self-awareness not only helps me understand them better but also empowers them to take control of their learning journey.

Remember, weaknesses aren't permanent obstacles; they're opportunities for growth. When we identify areas where a student struggles, we're not labeling them as deficient. Instead, we're pinpointing where they have the most potential for improvement.

- **From a Parent's Perspective:**

As a parent, you have a unique vantage point to observe your child's English language journey. You see their struggles and triumphs in real-world contexts outside the structured environment of the classroom. This perspective is invaluable in identifying your child's strengths and weaknesses in English.

Pay attention to how your child interacts with English in daily life. Do they confidently order for themselves at restaurants but shy away from writing emails? Are they glued to English language YouTube videos but struggle with reading English books? These observations can provide clues about their strengths and areas for improvement.

Engage in regular conversations with your child about their English learning. Ask them what they find easy or difficult and what they enjoy or dislike about learning English. Their responses can offer insights that might not be apparent from observation alone.

Keep an eye on your child's homework and school assignments. Which types of tasks do they complete quickly and easily? Which ones seem to cause frustration? This can help you identify patterns in their strengths and weaknesses.

Feel free to communicate with your child's teachers. They can provide professional insights into your child's performance across different language skills and may notice things that aren't apparent at home.

Remember, identifying weaknesses isn't about criticism; it's about understanding where your child needs extra support. Celebrate their strengths and approach areas of difficulty with a positive, growth-oriented mindset.

Personalized Strategies for Different Types of Learners

1. **From a Teacher's Perspective**

   - **Visual Learners:**

These students learn best through seeing. In my classroom, I cater to visual learners by using plenty of charts, graphs, and images. I might use color coding to teach grammar concepts or create mind maps to illustrate vocabulary relationships.

One effective strategy is the use of video resources. Short clips can be powerful tools for teaching everything from vocabulary to cultural concepts. I also encourage visual learners to create their visual aids, like flashcards or infographics, as the process of making these can reinforce their learning.

For writing tasks, I suggest providing graphic organizers to help visual learners structure their ideas. When teaching new vocabulary, I often pair words with images or encourage students to draw their representations.

   - **Auditory Learners:**

These students thrive on spoken information. For auditory learners, I incorporate plenty of listening exercises, discussions, and oral presentations into my lessons. I suggest using podcasts or audiobooks as teaching tools or creating opportunities for peer teaching where students explain concepts to each other.

Music can be a powerful tool for auditory learners. Songs can help with vocabulary retention, pronunciation practice, and even grammar concepts. I often use jazz chants or create simple tunes to help students remember tricky language rules.

For these learners, I might provide recorded instructions for assignments or encourage them to read their writing aloud as part of the editing process. Group work and oral discussions are also particularly beneficial for auditory learners.

- **Kinesthetic Learners:**

These are the "hands-on" learners who benefit from physical activity and tactile experiences. In my classroom, I incorporate movement and touch into lessons whenever possible. This might involve role-playing exercises for conversation practice, using manipulatives for grammar lessons, or incorporating Total Physical Response (TPR) methods where students act out vocabulary words.

For kinesthetic learners, I might set up "stations" around the classroom where students move from one activity to another. I also use games and physical activities to reinforce learning. For example, a grammar concept might be taught through a board game, or vocabulary could be practiced with a classroom scavenger hunt.

When teaching writing, I might have kinesthetic learners physically cut up and rearrange sentences to understand structure. For vocabulary, we might use Play-Doh to sculpt representations of words or act out verb tenses.

- **Reading/Writing Learners:**

These learners prefer the written word. I provide plenty of written materials and encourage note-taking. I use written quizzes or worksheets to reinforce concepts or assign journal writing for reflection on lessons.

For these learners, I often provide written summaries of key points from lessons. I encourage them to rewrite definitions in their own words or to create their example sentences for new vocabulary.

In group work, I might assign these learners the role of "scribe" to play to their strengths. For presentations, I might allow them to prepare written scripts.

2. **From a Parent's Perspective:**

- **Visual Learners:**

At home, you can support visual learners by providing plenty of visual materials. This might include English language picture books, flashcards, or educational posters. You could create a "word wall" in their room where new vocabulary is displayed visually.

Encourage your child to draw pictures to represent new words or concepts. When helping with homework, use diagrams or flowcharts to explain ideas. Watch English language videos together and discuss what you see.

For older children, encourage the use of highlighters or colored pens when studying to organize information visually. Mind mapping can be an excellent tool for visual learners to plan writing tasks or study for tests.

- **Auditory Learners:**

For auditory learners, the key is to provide plenty of opportunities to hear and speak English. This might involve listening to English language audiobooks or podcasts together or having regular English conversation time as a family.

Encourage your child to read aloud when studying or to record themselves speaking and listen back. You might play word games that focus on sounds, like rhyming games or "I Spy" with phonetic clues.

Music can be an excellent tool for auditory learners. Find English language songs that your child enjoys and sing along together. You might even make up silly songs to remember grammar rules or vocabulary.

- **Kinesthetic Learners:**

For these hands-on learners, try to make English practice as active as possible. This might involve acting out stories you read together, using gestures to remember new words, or playing active games that incorporate English skills.

Create tactile vocabulary cards where your child can trace the letters. Use manipulatives like Scrabble tiles for spelling practice.

For grammar practice, you might cut up sentences and have your child physically rearrange them.

Incorporate English into physical activities. This could be as simple as calling out vocabulary words for your child to act out or as elaborate as setting up an obstacle course with English instructions.

- **Reading/Writing Learners:**

These learners thrive on written materials. Encourage plenty of reading in English, from books to magazines to online articles. Keep a family journal where everyone writes entries in English.

Encourage your child to write summaries of English books they've read or movies they've watched. Play word games like crosswords or Scrabble. For vocabulary practice, have them write new words in sentences or stories.

When studying, please encourage your child to rewrite their notes or create their study guides. For younger children, you might create fill-in-the-blank stories together.

Regardless of learning style, the key is to make English practice a regular, enjoyable part of daily life. Be patient, celebrate progress, and always keep in mind that every child's language-learning journey is unique. By tailoring your approach to your child's individual needs and preferences, you're setting them up for success in their English language journey.

- Chapter 6 -
USING TECHNOLOGY TO ENHANCE ENGLISH LANGUAGE LEARNING

The digital revolution has transformed the landscape of education, and English language learning is no exception. In my years of teaching, I've witnessed a remarkable shift in how technology can enhance, accelerate, and personalize the language learning experience. Gone are the days when language acquisition was confined to textbooks and classrooms. Today, the world of English is at our fingertips, accessible through a myriad of digital platforms and tools.

Benefits of Incorporating Technology into ESL Education

The integration of technology into ESL education has opened up a world of once unimaginable possibilities. As an educator, I've seen firsthand how digital tools can breathe new life into language learning, making it more engaging, interactive, and relevant to today's learners.

One of the most significant benefits of technology in ESL education is the ability to provide authentic language exposure. In the past, students might have had limited access to native English speakers or real-world language use. Now, with just a few clicks, learners can immerse themselves in authentic English content from around the globe. They can watch news broadcasts, listen to podcasts, or engage in conversations with native speakers, all from the comfort of their homes or classrooms.

This exposure to authentic language is crucial for developing natural, fluent English skills. It helps students understand how English is really used in different contexts and cultures beyond the sometimes artificial scenarios presented in textbooks. I've seen students make remarkable progress in their listening comprehension and speaking skills simply by regularly engaging with authentic online content.

Another significant advantage of technology in ESL education is the opportunity for personalized learning. Digital platforms can adapt to a learner's pace, style, and level in ways that are difficult to achieve in a traditional classroom setting. Adaptive learning software can identify a student's strengths and weaknesses, providing targeted practice in areas that need improvement. This level of individualization can be a game-changer, especially for students who might feel left behind or unchallenged in a one-size-fits-all approach.

Technology also allows for immediate feedback, which is crucial in language learning. Many apps and online platforms can instantly correct pronunciation, grammar, or vocabulary errors, allowing students to make adjustments in real time. This immediate reinforcement can accelerate learning and help prevent the fossilization of mistakes.

The flexibility offered by technology is another significant benefit. ESL learners can now practice English anytime, anywhere. This is particularly valuable for adult learners who might be juggling work and family commitments. The ability to squeeze in a quick language lesson during a commute or lunch break can make consistent practice more achievable for busy individuals.

Moreover, technology can make language learning more engaging and interactive. Gamification elements in language learning apps can turn grammar drills or vocabulary practice into fun, competitive activities. Virtual reality and augmented reality technologies are beginning to offer immersive language experiences that can simulate real-world interactions. These engaging formats can boost motivation and make language learning feel less like a chore and more like an enjoyable activity.

Collaboration is another area where technology shines in ESL education. Online platforms can connect learners from around the world, allowing them to practice with peers, engage in cultural exchange, and build a global community of language learners. This not only provides opportunities for authentic language use but also fosters intercultural understanding and global citizenship.

For teachers, technology offers powerful tools for assessment and tracking student progress. Digital platforms can provide detailed analytics on student performance, helping teachers identify areas where students are struggling and tailor their instruction accordingly. This data-driven approach can lead to more effective teaching strategies and better outcomes for students.

Technology can also bridge the gap between classroom learning and real-world application. For instance, students can use language learning apps to prepare for an upcoming trip abroad or use translation tools to understand English content related to their hobbies or interests. This practical application can make language learning feel more relevant and motivating.

However, it's important to note that technology is not a panacea. It's a tool that, when used effectively, can significantly enhance the language learning experience. The key is to integrate technology in a thoughtful, purposeful way that complements rather than replaces traditional teaching methods. The most effective approach is a blended one that combines the best of both digital and traditional learning strategies.

Recommended Online Tools, Apps, and Resources

The digital marketplace is flooded with language learning tools and resources, which can be overwhelming for both educators and learners. Over the years, I've experimented with numerous platforms and have identified several that consistently deliver value for ESL learners. Here's a curated list of some of the most effective tools I've encountered:

- **Duolingo:** This free app offers a gamified approach to language learning. It's perfect for vocabulary building and essential grammar practice. The bite-sized lessons make it easy to maintain a daily learning habit, even for busy individuals.

- **Quizlet:** An excellent tool for vocabulary practice, Quizlet allows users to create their own flashcard sets or use those created by others. It offers various study modes, including games, which can make vocabulary review more engaging.

- **Grammarly:** While primarily a writing tool, Grammarly can be invaluable for ESL learners. It provides real-time grammar and spelling corrections, helping learners improve their writing skills. The explanations it offers for corrections can also serve as mini grammar lessons.

- **BBC Learning English:** This free resource offers a wealth of materials for ESL learners, including news-based lessons, vocabulary exercises, and pronunciation guides. It's handy for learners who want to improve their British English skills.

- **TED-Ed:** TED-Ed videos, with their engaging animations and diverse topics, can be excellent for listening practice and vocabulary expansion. Many videos come with interactive questions and discussion prompts, making them great for comprehension practice.

- **Tandem:** This language exchange app connects learners with native speakers for conversation practice. It's an excellent way to practice speaking skills and learn about different cultures.

- **Lyrics Training:** This website uses popular music videos to create gap-fill exercises, making it a fun way to practice listening skills and learn new vocabulary in context.

- **NewsELA:** This platform offers current news articles at various reading levels, making it easier for ESL learners to engage with authentic content without feeling overwhelmed.

- **VoiceThread:** This collaborative tool allows users to have asynchronous conversations around images, documents, or videos. It's great for speaking practice and can be used for class projects or presentations.

- **Kahoot!:** A game-based learning platform that can make review sessions fun and engaging. Teachers can create their quizzes or use existing ones.

For younger learners:

- **ABCmouse:** This comprehensive early learning platform includes ESL lessons for young children. It uses a curriculum-based approach with fun, interactive activities.

- **PBS Kids:** While not specifically for ESL, PBS Kids offers a variety of educational games and videos that can support English language development in a fun, age-appropriate way.

- **Stories by Gus on the Go:** This app offers interactive stories in multiple languages, helping children learn English through engaging narratives and activities.

For more advanced learners:

- **Readlang:** This web reader allows users to click on unfamiliar words to see translations while reading authentic web content. It's great for expanding vocabulary in context.

- **Youglish:** This tool uses YouTube videos to show how words are pronounced in context. It's excellent for improving pronunciation and understanding how words are used naturally.

- **Hemingway Editor:** While not explicitly designed for ESL learners, this writing tool can help advanced learners improve their writing style by identifying complex sentences, passive voice, and other stylistic issues.

These tools can be incredibly effective, but it's essential to use them as part of a balanced language-learning approach. They should complement, not replace, other forms of language practice and instruction. Encourage learners to experiment with different tools to find what works best for their learning style and goals.

Safely Navigating the Online Learning Landscape

While the digital world offers incredible opportunities for language learning, it also comes with potential risks and challenges. As educators and parents, we must guide learners in navigating this landscape safely and effectively.

First and foremost, online safety should be a priority. When recommending online tools or platforms, especially for younger learners, always ensure they have strong privacy policies and age-appropriate content. Teach learners about the importance of protecting their personal information online and how to recognize potential online dangers.

It's also essential to verify the credibility of online learning resources. Not all language learning content on the internet is created equal. Look for platforms developed by reputable educational organizations or language experts. Be wary of sites that make unrealistic promises about rapid language acquisition.

When it comes to choosing appropriate learning platforms, consider the learner's age, proficiency level, and learning goals. A platform that works well for an adult business professional might not be suitable for a young child just starting to learn English. Look for platforms that offer placement tests or adaptive learning features to ensure the content is at an appropriate level.

Encourage a balanced approach to online learning. While digital tools can be incredibly effective, they should only partially replace human interaction in language learning. Combine online practice with opportunities for real-world language use and face-to-face communication.

Be mindful of screen time, especially for younger learners. While digital tools can be engaging, excessive screen time can have adverse effects. Set reasonable limits and encourage breaks for physical activity or offline learning activities.

Teach critical thinking skills when it comes to online content. Not all information found online is accurate or reliable. Encourage learners to cross-reference information and to be discerning about the sources they trust for language learning.

For parents, it's essential to stay involved in your child's online learning activities. Regularly check in on what platforms they're using and how they're progressing. Many learning apps have parent portals that allow you to monitor your child's activity and progress.

Consider the potential for distraction in online learning environments. While the internet offers a wealth of resources, it can also be a source of distraction. Teach strategies for staying focused during online learning sessions, such as using website blockers or setting specific study times.

Be aware of the potential for online fatigue. Spending prolonged periods engaged in online learning can be mentally taxing. Encourage regular breaks and a mix of online and offline learning activities to maintain engagement and prevent burnout.

Finally, remember that technology should enhance, not replace, the human element in language learning. The most effective online tools are those that facilitate honest communication and cultural exchange. Look for platforms that offer opportunities for interaction with native speakers or other language learners.

Technology has revolutionized the way we approach ESL education, offering unprecedented opportunities for personalized, engaging, and effective language learning. By thoughtfully incorporating digital tools into our teaching and learning strategies, we can create rich, multifaceted language learning experiences that prepare learners for using English in the real world. However, it's crucial to approach online learning with a critical eye, prioritizing safety, credibility, and balance in our digital language learning journey.

When used wisely, technology can be a powerful ally in our quest to empower English learners and open up a world of opportunities through language acquisition.

- Chapter 7 -
FOSTERING A LOVE FOR READING AND WRITING IN ENGLISH

The written word holds a unique power to transport, transform, and transcend. In my journey as an ESL educator, I've witnessed countless moments where the spark of language ignites through the pages of a book or the stroke of a pen. This chapter is dedicated to nurturing that spark into a roaring flame of passion for English reading and writing.

The Importance of Reading and Writing Skills in Mastering English Language Proficiency

Reading and writing form the bedrock of language mastery. They are the silent skills that speak volumes about a learner's proficiency. When we read, we absorb the rhythm and flow of English, internalizing grammar structures and vocabulary in context. It's a process of linguistic osmosis, where learners soak up the nuances of the language almost effortlessly.

The impact of regular reading on language acquisition is profound. It exposes learners to a wide range of vocabulary, idiomatic expressions, and sentence structures that they might not encounter in everyday conversation. This expanded linguistic repertoire then seeps into their own language use, enriching their speaking and writing.

Moreover, reading in English opens doors to new worlds of knowledge and culture. It's not just about language acquisition; it's about gaining access to a global repository of ideas and perspectives. Through English literature, learners can explore diverse cultures, historical periods, and ways of thinking. This cultural literacy is an invaluable asset in our interconnected world.

Writing, on the other hand, is the crucible where language knowledge is tested and refined. When we write, we actively engage with the language, making choices about vocabulary, syntax, and style. This process of active language production cements learning in a way that passive consumption cannot match.

The act of writing forces learners to organize their thoughts coherently in English, a skill that translates directly to more articulate speech. It's a form of linguistic problem-solving, where learners must figure out how to express complex ideas within the constraints of their current language abilities. This challenge pushes them to expand their language skills, driving progress in all areas of language proficiency.

Furthermore, writing provides a tangible record of a learner's progress. Looking back at earlier writing samples can be incredibly motivating, as learners can clearly see how far they've come. This sense of achievement fuels further effort, creating a positive cycle of improvement.

The synergy between reading and writing is particularly powerful. Reading provides input - exposure to authentic language use - while writing allows for output, the active application of acquired knowledge. This input-output cycle is crucial for deep, lasting language acquisition.

In our digital age, strong English reading and writing skills are more important than ever. From professional emails to social media posts, written English is often the primary mode of communication in global contexts. By developing these skills, we're equipping ESL learners with tools that will serve them well in their academic, professional, and personal lives.

It's worth noting that the benefits of developing strong reading and writing skills in English extend beyond language proficiency. These skills foster critical thinking, creativity, and emotional intelligence. They allow learners to engage with complex ideas, express their own thoughts and feelings, and empathize with diverse perspectives.

As educators and parents, our role is to create an environment where reading and writing in English are not seen as chores, but as gateways to discovery and self-expression. When we succeed in fostering a love for these skills, we're not just teaching language; we're empowering learners to find their voice in a global conversation.

Engaging Reading Materials and Writing Prompts for Different Proficiency Levels

Selecting appropriate reading materials and crafting engaging writing prompts is an art form in itself. The goal is to challenge learners without overwhelming them, to spark interest while expanding horizons. Here's a guide to materials and prompts tailored to different proficiency levels:

For beginners, the key is to build confidence and vocabulary through accessible, visually engaging materials. Picture books are invaluable at this stage. They provide visual context for new words and often feature repetitive text that reinforces basic sentence structures. Some excellent choices include "The Very Hungry Caterpillar" by Eric Carle, which introduces days of the week and food vocabulary, or "Brown Bear, Brown Bear, What Do You See?" by Bill Martin Jr., which focuses on colors and animals.

Writing prompts for beginners should be concrete and relate to their immediate experiences. Asking them to describe their favorite toy, write about their family, or recount their day uses familiar vocabulary while encouraging self-expression. The focus here is on communicating ideas, not grammatical perfection.

As learners progress to an intermediate level, they can handle more complex narratives and a wider range of vocabulary. Chapter books with engaging plots and relatable characters are ideal. The "Magic Tree House" series by Mary Pope Osborne, for instance, combines adventure with historical and scientific facts, expanding both language skills and general knowledge.

For non-fiction at this level, National Geographic Kids publications offer engaging content with strong visual support. These materials introduce academic vocabulary in accessible contexts, preparing learners for more advanced studies.

Writing prompts for intermediate learners can be more open-ended and imaginative. Asking them to write a letter to their future self, describe their dream vacation, or create a new ending for a familiar story encourages creativity while practicing more complex sentence structures.

Advanced learners are ready for the richness of young adult literature and even some classic works. Books like "The Giver" by Lois Lowry or "To Kill a Mockingbird" by Harper Lee offer complex themes and sophisticated language use. These texts not only improve language skills but also foster critical thinking and cultural understanding.

For non-fiction, books on current events, science, or history can expand vocabulary and knowledge in specific areas of interest. Magazines like "Time for Kids" or "The Week Junior" provide age-appropriate coverage of global issues.

Writing prompts for advanced learners can be quite sophisticated. They might be asked to argue for or against a controversial topic, analyze the themes in a book they've read, or write a story from an unusual perspective. The goal is to encourage nuanced thinking and stylistic experimentation.

Across all levels, it's crucial to consider learners' interests. A reluctant reader might be more likely to engage with a book about their favorite sport or hobby. Similarly, writing prompts that connect to learners' personal experiences or passions are more likely to inspire enthusiastic responses.

Online resources can be valuable supplements to traditional materials. Websites like Newsela offer current events articles at multiple reading levels, allowing learners to engage with real-world content appropriate to their proficiency. For writing, platforms like Storybird can inspire creativity by allowing students to write stories based on beautiful illustrations.

The key is to provide a diverse range of materials and prompts that cater to different interests and learning styles. Some learners might prefer graphic novels, while others might enjoy poetry. Some might thrive on factual writing, while others lose themselves in fantasy worlds. By offering variety, we increase the chances of each learner finding their own path to English literacy.

Tips for Parents to Cultivate a Love for Reading and Writing in Their Child

Parents are the unsung heroes of language education. Their influence extends far beyond the classroom, shaping attitudes and habits that can last a lifetime. Here are some strategies for parents to nurture a love of reading and writing in English:

Create a print-rich environment. Surround your child with English books, magazines, and other reading materials. Make them easily accessible and visible in your home. This constant exposure normalizes English reading and sparks curiosity. Even if you're not a confident English speaker yourself, having these materials around sends a powerful message about the value of English literacy.

Establish a family reading routine. Set aside time each day for reading together. For younger children, this might involve reading aloud, using different voices for characters to bring the story to life. For older children, try partner reading where you take turns reading pages. Even if you're still learning English yourself, this shared experience can be valuable for both of you.

Be a role model. Let your child see you engaging with English texts. Whether you're reading a novel, a newspaper, or even just product labels at the grocery store, your example shows that English reading is a normal, valuable part of daily life.

Make library visits a special event. Regular trips to the library can be exciting for children. Allow them to choose their own books - having control over their reading material can increase engagement. Many libraries also offer English storytimes or reading clubs, which can provide additional motivation and social interaction around reading.

Leverage technology wisely. E-books and reading apps can be engaging for tech-savvy kids. Platforms like Epic! offer a wide range of digital books for different ages and interests. However, balance this with physical books to provide a multi-sensory reading experience.

Connect reading to real life. If you're planning a family outing, read books related to your destination beforehand. This makes reading feel relevant and exciting. For instance, before a trip to the zoo, you might read books about animals together.

Start a family book club. For older children, choose a book to read as a family and discuss it together. This not only encourages reading but also develops critical thinking and conversation skills in English.

Celebrate writing. Display your child's English writing prominently in your home. This could be stories, poems, or even just well-written sentences. Seeing their work valued can be a huge motivator.

Engage in family writing activities. This could involve crafting stories together, keeping a family journal, or writing letters to relatives. These shared experiences make writing feel like a fun, social activity rather than a solitary chore.

Provide authentic writing opportunities. Encourage your child to write shopping lists, thank-you notes, or emails to friends in

English. This shows the practical value of writing skills and provides real-world motivation for improvement.

Be patient and positive. Learning to read and write in a new language takes time. Praise effort and progress, not just results. A positive, encouraging atmosphere can make all the difference in maintaining motivation.

Explore different genres. Expose your child to various types of reading materials - fiction, non-fiction, poetry, comics. This variety can help them discover what they enjoy most and prevents boredom.

Use multimedia to support reading. Pair books with their movie adaptations, or listen to audiobooks together. This multi-sensory approach can enhance understanding and enjoyment, especially for learners who might struggle with traditional reading.

Encourage journaling. Suggest that your child keeps a diary in English. This private, low-pressure writing can help them become more comfortable expressing themselves in English and provides regular writing practice.

Connect with other English-learning families. Look for or create a community of families on a similar language journey. This could involve organizing English book clubs for children or participating in language exchange events. Peer interaction can make reading and writing more engaging and provide additional motivation.

The key to all these strategies is to make reading and writing in English enjoyable, not a chore. Every child is different, so be prepared to try different approaches until you find what works best for your child. The goal is to spark a lifelong love of reading and writing that will serve them well in their English language journey and beyond.

By fostering a love for reading and writing in English, we're not just helping ESL learners improve their language skills. We're opening doors to new worlds, ideas, and possibilities. We're giving them tools to express themselves, to understand others, and to engage with a global community. In a world where communication is key, these are truly invaluable gifts.

- Chapter 8 -
OVERCOMING CHALLENGES AND CELEBRATING PROGRESS

The path of language learning is rarely a straight line. It's more akin to a winding road, filled with unexpected turns, steep climbs, and occasionally, moments where we feel like we're going backwards. Yet, it's precisely these challenges that make the journey of learning English so rewarding. In my years of working with ESL learners and their families, I've come to appreciate that every obstacle overcome is a victory worth celebrating, and every setback is an opportunity for growth.

Common Roadblocks for ESL Learners and Their Parents

One of the most pervasive challenges I've encountered is the ebb and flow of motivation. It's natural for enthusiasm to wane at times, especially when progress seems slow or the task at hand feels overwhelming. For children, this might manifest as reluctance to practice English at home or disengagement in class. Parents, too, can experience motivational dips, particularly if they're learning alongside their children and feeling the weight of their own language struggles.

Another significant hurdle is the language barrier itself. For students, this can lead to frustration when they struggle to express complex thoughts or understand nuanced instructions. It's not uncommon for ESL learners to feel a sense of dual identity, caught between their native language and English, sometimes not feeling fully proficient in either. This can impact self-esteem and willingness to take risks with the language.

Parents often face their own set of language-related challenges. Many feel ill-equipped to support their child's English learning, especially if their own English skills are limited. This can lead to a sense of helplessness or even guilt. Additionally, language barriers can make it difficult for parents to communicate effectively with teachers or fully engage in their child's school community.

Cultural differences can also pose significant challenges. ESL learners and their families may find themselves navigating unfamiliar social norms and educational expectations. This cultural dissonance can lead to misunderstandings and feelings of isolation. Moreover, the pressure to assimilate can sometimes conflict with the desire to maintain one's cultural identity, creating internal tension for both children and parents.

Time management is another common roadblock. Many ESL students are juggling language learning with regular academic subjects, often resulting in a heavy workload. For parents, finding time to support their child's English learning amidst busy work schedules and family responsibilities can be daunting.

The fear of making mistakes is a particularly insidious challenge. I've seen countless students hesitate to speak or write in English because they're afraid of errors. This fear can severely hamper progress, as language learning requires active practice and a willingness to take risks.

For some families, limited access to resources can be a significant obstacle. This might include a lack of English-language materials at home, limited internet access for online learning tools, or financial constraints that prevent participation in additional language programs or tutoring.

Lastly, unrealistic expectations can be a major roadblock. Some learners and parents expect rapid fluency, and when progress is slower than anticipated, discouragement sets in. This can lead to a cycle of frustration and decreased motivation.

Practical Solutions and Strategies for Overcoming Challenges

Addressing these challenges requires a multifaceted approach, combining practical strategies with a shift in mindset. Here are some solutions I've found effective:

To combat fluctuating motivation, it's crucial to set realistic, achievable goals. Break down the language learning journey into smaller, manageable steps. Celebrate each milestone, no matter how small. This could be mastering a new grammar point, reading a book in English without translation, or having a successful conversation with a native speaker. By acknowledging these incremental successes, we maintain a sense of progress and momentum.

Creating a supportive learning environment is key. This might involve establishing a regular study routine, designating a specific area in the home for English practice, or joining a community of other ESL learners for mutual support. For parents, this could mean setting aside time for family English activities, even if it's just 15 minutes a day of reading together or watching an English-language show.

To address the language barrier, immersion is crucial, but it needs to be tailored to the learner's level to avoid overwhelm. Start with English content that's just slightly above the current level of proficiency. This could be graded readers, podcasts designed for English learners, or TV shows with English subtitles. Gradually increase the difficulty as confidence grows.

For parents struggling with their own English skills, it's important to emphasize that perfect fluency isn't necessary to support their child's learning. Simple activities like learning new English words together, practicing pronunciation as a family, or even just showing interest in their child's English studies can have a significant impact. Many schools and community centers offer English classes for parents, which can be a great way to improve skills and better support their children.

Addressing cultural differences requires open dialogue and cultural sensitivity. Encourage ESL learners and their families to share their cultural experiences and perspectives. This not only helps them feel valued but also enriches the learning environment for everyone. For teachers, incorporating diverse cultural elements into lessons can help students feel more connected to the material.

Time management challenges can be addressed through prioritization and efficient study techniques. Teaching students how to use time-blocking, the Pomodoro technique, or other time management strategies can help them balance language learning with other responsibilities. For parents, integrating English practice into daily routines (like discussing the day in English during dinner) can make it feel less like an additional task.

To combat the fear of making mistakes, it's crucial to foster a positive attitude towards errors. Emphasize that mistakes are a natural and necessary part of the learning process. Create low-stakes opportunities for language practice, like casual conversation clubs or writing journals that won't be graded. Modeling this attitude as a teacher or parent – being willing to make and laugh at your own language mistakes – can be incredibly powerful.

For families with limited resources, creativity is key. Utilize free online resources like language learning apps, YouTube videos, public library materials, or platform-provided materials, such as

Schoolization's free resource offerings. These resources offer accessible ways to supplement learning and keep students engaged outside of formal lessons. Community resources like language exchange meetups or volunteer-led ESL programs can also be valuable. Teachers can support by providing information about these resources and, where possible, offering materials that can be used at home.

Addressing unrealistic expectations involves education and perspective-shifting. Help learners and parents understand the typical timeline for language acquisition and the natural plateaus that occur. Share success stories of other ESL learners to provide inspiration and realistic models of progress.

Throughout all of these strategies, maintaining a positive, growth-oriented mindset is crucial. Emphasize that language learning is a journey, not a destination. Every challenge overcome is a step forward, even if it doesn't feel like it in the moment.

Celebrating Small Victories and Milestones

In the marathon of language learning, it's the small victories that fuel our progress. As educators and parents, one of our most important roles is to recognize and celebrate these achievements, no matter how minor they might seem.

First, it's important to redefine what we consider a "victory" in language learning. It's not just about acing tests or achieving perfect pronunciation. Victories can be as simple as using a new word correctly in conversation, understanding a joke in English, or having the courage to order at a restaurant in English for the first time. By broadening our definition of success, we create more opportunities for positive reinforcement.

Creating a visual representation of progress can be incredibly motivating. This could be a language learning journey map on the wall, where milestones are marked with stickers or photos. For younger learners, a sticker chart for completed English activities can provide a tangible sense of achievement. Older students might keep a language learning journal, where they can reflect on their progress and see how far they've come.

Celebration doesn't always have to be grand. Sometimes, a simple acknowledgment is powerful. This could be a high-five for using a difficult phrasal verb correctly, or a special note in a child's homework recognizing their effort. The key is consistency – regularly noticing and commenting on progress, no matter how small.

Incorporating fun into milestone celebrations can associate positive emotions with language learning. This might involve a special family outing after completing an English book, watching a favorite English movie as a reward for a week of consistent practice, or having a "English only" day where the whole family challenges themselves to communicate solely in English.

It's also valuable to celebrate effort, not just results. Recognize when a learner pushes through a challenging task, even if the outcome isn't perfect. This fosters a growth mindset and resilience, crucial qualities for long-term language learning success.

Involving the wider community in celebrations can provide additional motivation and support. This could mean sharing achievements with extended family members, posting progress updates on a class blog, or participating in school-wide language learning events where students can showcase their skills.

For parents, it's important to celebrate their own progress too, especially if they're learning alongside their children. This models the idea that language learning is a lifelong journey and that every step forward is valuable, regardless of age or starting point.

Encourage reflection as part of the celebration process. Help learners articulate what they've achieved and how it makes them feel. This metacognitive practice not only reinforces the sense of accomplishment but also helps learners identify effective strategies they can apply to future challenges.

The journey of learning English is filled with both challenges and triumphs. By acknowledging the roadblocks, implementing practical strategies to overcome them, and consciously celebrating every step forward, we create an environment where language learning becomes not just achievable, but enjoyable. As educators and parents, our role is to guide, support, and cheer from the sidelines, recognizing that each learner's path is unique and valuable. In doing so, we're not just teaching a language; we're fostering resilience, curiosity, and a lifelong love of learning. These are skills that will serve our ESL learners well, not just in their language journey, but in all aspects of their lives.

- Chapter 9 -
CREATING A SUPPORTIVE LEARNING COMMUNITY

The journey of language acquisition is rarely a solitary one. In my years of experience in ESL education, I've come to understand that the most successful learners are often those surrounded by a robust network of support. This network acts as a safety net, a cheering squad, and a source of shared wisdom. It's the collective effort of educators, parents, peers, and community members that truly empowers English learners to reach their full potential.

The Importance of Building a Supportive Network

Imagine trying to climb a mountain alone versus ascending with a team of experienced climbers. The solo climber might eventually reach the summit, but the journey would be infinitely more challenging, fraught with unnecessary risks and missed opportunities for growth. This analogy perfectly encapsulates the importance of a supportive network in ESL learning.

A well-constructed support system serves multiple crucial functions. First and foremost, it provides emotional support.

Learning a new language can be an emotionally taxing experience, filled with moments of frustration, self-doubt, and cultural disorientation. Having a network of individuals who understand these challenges can provide the encouragement and empathy needed to persevere through difficult times.

Moreover, a diverse support network expands the opportunities for authentic language practice. While classroom instruction is invaluable, it's in real-world interactions that language skills are truly honed. A supportive community can provide varied contexts for English use, from casual conversations with peers to more formal interactions with educators and community members.

From an educational perspective, a strong network can significantly enhance the learning process. When educators, parents, and peers are all aligned in their support of an ESL learner, it creates a cohesive learning environment that extends beyond the classroom walls. This continuity of support can reinforce lessons, provide multiple perspectives on language use, and create a more immersive English-learning experience.

For parents of ESL learners, a support network can be particularly empowering. Many parents feel ill-equipped to assist their children in English learning, especially if they are not confident English speakers themselves. A supportive community can provide resources, share strategies, and offer reassurance that they are not alone in their challenges.

Peer support within this network is equally crucial. ESL learners often feel isolated, particularly in mainstream educational settings. Connecting with peers who are on similar language journeys can provide a sense of belonging and mutual understanding. These peer relationships can also foster a spirit of healthy competition and collaboration, motivating learners to push their language skills further.

From a cultural perspective, a diverse support network can ease the process of acculturation that often accompanies language learning. It can provide a bridge between the learner's home culture and the target language culture, helping to navigate cultural differences and misunderstandings. This cultural support is invaluable in helping ESL learners develop not just language proficiency, but also the intercultural competence necessary for true global citizenship.

Furthermore, a robust support network can open doors to opportunities that might otherwise be inaccessible to individual learners or families. This could include information about scholarships, enrichment programs, or cultural events that can enhance the language learning experience.

In essence, building a supportive network transforms the ESL journey from a potentially isolating experience into a communal adventure. It creates a microcosm of the global, interconnected world that English proficiency aims to access. By fostering these connections, we're not just supporting language acquisition; we're building a community of lifelong learners and cultural ambassadors.

Tips for Connecting with Other ESL Families

Creating connections with other ESL families can be a game-changer in the language learning journey. These relationships provide a source of shared experiences, practical advice, and emotional support. However, initiating these connections can sometimes feel daunting, especially for families who are new to a community or those dealing with language barriers. Here are some strategies I've found effective in fostering these vital connections:

Start with your child's school. Many schools with ESL programs organize events specifically for ESL families. These might include orientation sessions, cultural celebrations, or parent workshops. Attending these events is an excellent way to meet other families in similar situations. Don't hesitate to introduce yourself to other parents, even if there's a language barrier. Often, a smile and a simple greeting can be the first step towards a supportive friendship.

Look for community-based organizations that serve immigrant or multilingual populations. These organizations often host social events, language classes, or support groups where you can meet other ESL families. They can also be valuable resources for information about local services and opportunities.

Utilize social media and online platforms. Facebook groups for ESL learners or local international communities can be great places to connect virtually with other families. Websites like Meetup.com often have groups dedicated to language exchange or multicultural friendships. These online connections can then transition into real-world relationships.

Consider starting a group yourself. If you can't find an existing group that meets your needs, consider initiating one. This could be as simple as a monthly coffee meetup for ESL parents at a local cafe, or a playgroup for children from multilingual families. You might be surprised at how many other families are looking for the same connections.

Participate in local events and classes. Library story times, community festivals, or adult education classes can be excellent places to meet other families. Even if these aren't specifically geared towards ESL learners, they provide opportunities to practice English and make connections in a relaxed setting.

Volunteer at your child's school or in community organizations. This not only helps you meet other parents but also allows you to model community involvement for your child. Many schools need volunteers for events, field trips, or classroom assistance, and this can be a great way to build relationships while supporting your child's education.

Organize language exchange meetups. If you're comfortable with your native language, consider organizing meetups where you can help others learn your language while practicing English. This reciprocal arrangement can lead to deep, meaningful connections.

Attend parent-teacher conferences and school board meetings. These events provide opportunities to meet other involved parents and to voice the needs and concerns of ESL families in your school community.

Look for cultural associations related to your home country or region. These groups often organize events that can help you maintain connections to your cultural heritage while also meeting other families navigating similar cultural and linguistic journeys.

Participate in sports or hobby groups. Joining a local sports team or hobby club can help you meet people with shared interests. While these groups might not be specifically for ESL families, shared activities can break down language barriers and lead to supportive friendships.

When making these connections, it's important to approach them with an open mind and a willingness to step out of your comfort zone. Language barriers can initially seem intimidating, but most people appreciate the effort to connect, even if communication isn't perfect.

Once you've made connections with other ESL families, nurture these relationships. Share resources you've found helpful, exchange tips on navigating the local school system, or simply offer a listening ear when challenges arise. These shared experiences can form the foundation of lasting, supportive friendships that enrich your family's ESL journey.

Guidance on Seeking Additional Support

While a supportive community of peers is invaluable, there are times when more specialized or intensive support may be beneficial. Recognizing when and how to seek this additional support can significantly enhance an ESL learner's progress and overall experience. Here's some guidance on exploring these additional resources:

English Teacher services can provide personalized attention that addresses specific learning needs. When considering a tutor, look for someone with ESL teaching experience and, ideally, familiarity with your child's native language or cultural background. Many schools offer after-school tutoring programs, or you might find independent tutors through local education centers or online platforms. Before committing to a tutor, consider arranging a trial session to ensure it's a good fit for your child's needs and learning style.

Language exchange programs offer a unique opportunity to practice English while also helping someone else learn your native language. These exchanges can be arranged through online platforms like Tandem or HelloTalk, or through local community organizations. For children, supervised language exchange playgroups can provide a fun, low-pressure environment for language practice.

Summer and winter language camps or immersion programs can provide intensive language practice in a fun, engaging setting. These programs often combine language instruction with cultural activities, sports, or arts and crafts. While they can be a significant investment, they offer the benefit of full immersion and the opportunity to make friends with other language learners.

Online learning platforms like Schoolization, Duolingo, Rosetta Stone, or BBC Learning English offer flexible, self-paced learning options. Platforms like these can be particularly useful for supplementary practice or for families with busy schedules. Many of these resources, including Schoolization, provide free versions or trial options so families can explore what works best before committing to a full program.

Community college courses can be an excellent resource for older learners or parents looking to improve their English skills. These courses often offer flexible scheduling and may be more affordable than private language schools. Additionally, many community colleges offer family literacy programs that provide simultaneous instruction for parents and children.

Public libraries often offer free or low-cost ESL resources. These might include conversation groups, storytimes for ESL families, or access to language learning software. Libraries can also be a source of free English reading materials at various levels, crucial for developing reading skills and vocabulary.

Volunteer conversation partners can provide opportunities for casual, real-world language practice. Many community organizations and universities have programs that match ESL learners with native English speakers for regular conversation practice. These partnerships can not only improve language skills but also foster cross-cultural friendships.

Professional development workshops for parents can provide strategies for supporting your child's language learning at home. Look for workshops offered by schools, libraries, or community organizations. These might cover topics like helping with English homework, creating a language-rich home environment, or understanding the local education system.

Speech and language therapists can provide specialized support for learners struggling with specific aspects of English, such as pronunciation or language processing. If you suspect your child might benefit from this type of support, consult with their ESL teacher or school counselor for a referral.

Cultural adjustment counseling can be beneficial for families struggling with the emotional and psychological aspects of learning a new language and adapting to a new culture. Many immigrant support organizations offer these services, often on a sliding scale based on income.

When seeking additional support, it's important to consider your family's specific needs, schedule, and budget. What works for one learner or family may not be the best fit for another. Be open to trying different options and adjusting your approach as needed.

Also, don't underestimate the value of creating your own support systems. This might involve forming a study group with other ESL learners, organizing a weekly English movie night with other families, or starting a book club that reads English books together. These self-organized support systems can be tailored to your specific needs and interests.

Seeking additional support is not a sign of failure or inadequacy. Rather, it's a proactive step towards maximizing learning opportunities and ensuring the best possible outcomes for ESL learners. By tapping into these additional resources, you're providing a richer, more diverse language learning experience that can accelerate progress and boost confidence.

Creating a supportive learning community is about weaving a web of connections and resources that collectively lift and empower ESL learners. It's about recognizing that language learning is not just an academic endeavor, but a holistic experience that touches every aspect of a learner's life. By building strong networks, fostering connections with other ESL families, and strategically seeking additional support, we create an environment where English learners can thrive, not just in their language skills, but as confident, well-rounded individuals ready to engage with the global community. This supportive ecosystem turns the challenges of language learning into opportunities for growth, cultural exchange, and lasting friendships. In doing so, we're not just teaching a language; we're building a community of global citizens, one supportive connection at a time.

- Chapter 10 -
FOR PARENTS - NURTURING YOUR CHILD'S ENGLISH VOCABULARY

The fabric of language is woven with words, each one a thread that adds color, texture, and meaning to our communication. As a parent supporting an ESL learner, you hold the unique position of being able to embroider this linguistic tapestry daily, in the comfort of your home and through the routines of family life. Expanding your child's English vocabulary isn't just about memorizing lists of words; it's about bringing language to life, making it relevant, enjoyable, and an integral part of your child's world.

In my years of working with ESL families, I've seen firsthand how a rich vocabulary can transform a child's confidence and competence in English. It's the key that unlocks more complex texts, enables nuanced expression, and opens doors to deeper cultural understanding. But I've also witnessed the struggles and frustrations that can come with vocabulary learning. That's why I'm passionate about sharing strategies that make this process not just effective, but genuinely enjoyable for both parents and children.

The Power of Shared Reading

One of the most potent tools in your vocabulary-building arsenal is the simple act of reading together. This isn't just about sitting side by side with a book; it's about creating a shared experience of language discovery. When you read with your child, you're not just exposing them to new words; you're providing context, pronunciation, and most importantly, a positive association with English language exploration.

Start by selecting books that are slightly above your child's current reading level. This 'stretch' is where vocabulary growth happens. As you read, pause to discuss unfamiliar words. Ask your child to guess the meaning based on the context or the pictures. This guessing game turns vocabulary learning into a fun challenge rather than a chore.

Don't shy away from more complex texts, even for younger children. Picture books often contain rich, descriptive language that can significantly boost vocabulary. For older children, try reading newspaper articles or short stories together. The key is to make it interactive – ask questions, encourage predictions, and relate the content to your child's experiences.

Consider creating a 'word wall' in your home where you can display new words discovered during your reading sessions. This visual reinforcement keeps the vocabulary alive beyond the pages of the book. Revisit these words regularly, perhaps making a game of using them in daily conversations.

Gamifying Vocabulary Learning

The power of play in language learning cannot be overstated. When we engage in games, our brains are more receptive to new information, and the emotional connection to the learning experience makes it more memorable. There's a wealth of word games that can turn vocabulary practice into family fun time.

Crossword puzzles are excellent for reinforcing spelling and understanding definitions. For younger children, create simple crosswords using words they're learning. Older children might enjoy tackling puzzles from newspapers or puzzle books. Make it a family activity, working together to solve clues and discuss new words as you encounter them.

Word searches can be particularly effective for visual learners. They help with word recognition and spelling. You can easily create custom word searches online based on the vocabulary your child is currently learning. For an extra challenge, don't provide a word list – have your child circle any English words they recognize.

Scrabble, or its digital equivalent Words with Friends, is a classic for a reason. It encourages players to recall and spell words, and also introduces the strategic element of word placement. For younger children, consider Junior Scrabble or allow the use of a dictionary to level the playing field.

'Categories' is a simple yet effective game that can be played anywhere. Choose a category (e.g., animals, foods, emotions) and take turns naming items in that category. This not only builds vocabulary but also helps with categorization and quick recall.

For a more active game, try 'Simon Says' with a vocabulary twist. Use it to practice body parts, actions, or positional words. "Simon says point to your elbow," or "Simon says walk perpendicular to the wall."

The Art of Visual Learning

Many children are visual learners, and tapping into this can supercharge vocabulary acquisition. Flashcards are a tried-and-true method, but let's take them to the next level. Instead of just writing the word and definition, include a picture or symbol that represents the word. Better yet, have your child draw the picture – the act of creating a visual representation cements the word in memory.

Take this visual approach further by labeling items around your house in English. This constant visual exposure to English words in their real-world context is incredibly powerful. Make it a family project to create and decorate these labels together.

For more advanced learners, try creating mind maps or word webs. Start with a central word or concept and branch out with related words. This not only builds vocabulary but also helps understand word relationships and associations.

Embracing Technology for Vocabulary Enhancement

In our digital age, technology offers myriad opportunities for vocabulary building. Language learning apps can turn practice into an addictive game. Apps like Duolingo or Memrise use spaced repetition and gamification to make vocabulary stick.

However, it's crucial to use these apps as supplements rather than primary learning tools. Set aside time to explore new words learned through apps together, discussing their meanings and using them in sentences.

Educational websites can also be valuable resources. Websites like Vocabulary.com or Freerice.com offer adaptive vocabulary practice that adjusts to your child's level. Many of these sites have game-like interfaces that make learning engaging.

For a more immersive experience, consider using English language voice assistants like Siri or Alexa. Encourage your child to ask questions or give commands in English. This not only practices vocabulary but also pronunciation and sentence structure.

The Power of Personal Connection

One of the most effective ways to make vocabulary stick is to make it personally relevant. Encourage your child to keep a personal word journal. This isn't just a list of words and definitions – it's a place for your child to write sentences using the new words, draw pictures, or note where they encountered the word.

Create themed word lists based on your child's interests. If they're passionate about soccer, create a list of sports-related vocabulary. If they love cooking, explore kitchen and food-related words. By connecting vocabulary to their interests, you're making the words more meaningful and memorable.

Contextual learning is key. Instead of learning words in isolation, focus on using them in real-life situations. If you're at the grocery store, discuss the names of fruits and vegetables. If you're cooking together, read the recipe aloud and explain any unfamiliar terms. These real-world connections make the vocabulary more likely to stick.

Celebrating Progress and Maintaining Motivation

Learning new vocabulary is a journey, not a destination. It's important to celebrate progress along the way. Consider creating a 'Word of the Week' tradition in your family. Choose a new word each week, display it prominently, and challenge family members to use it as often as possible. At the end of the week, share favorite sentences or moments using the word.

Maintain motivation by setting achievable goals. This could be learning a certain number of new words each week or reading a book slightly above their current level. Celebrate when these goals are met – perhaps with a special outing or a favorite meal.

Remember that mistakes are a natural and necessary part of the learning process. Create an atmosphere where it's okay to experiment with new words, even if they're not used perfectly. Praise effort and creativity in language use.

The Importance of Consistent Exposure

Consistency is key in vocabulary building. Aim to incorporate some form of vocabulary practice into each day, even if it's just for a few minutes. This could be as simple as having an 'English hour' where the family tries to communicate only in English, or a bedtime ritual of sharing new words learned that day.

Encourage your child to read independently in English as well. Provide a variety of reading materials – books, magazines, comics, even appropriate websites. The more diverse the reading material, the more varied the vocabulary exposure will be.

Leading by Example

As a parent, one of the most powerful things you can do is model a love of language and learning. Share new words you've learned, express excitement about interesting phrases you've encountered, and demonstrate how you use context clues to understand unfamiliar words when you're reading.

If you're learning English alongside your child, be open about your own learning process. Share your challenges and successes. This not only normalizes the learning process but also creates a shared experience that can bring you closer together.

Building your child's English vocabulary is a multifaceted process that can be woven into the fabric of daily life. By combining structured learning with playful exploration, leveraging technology while maintaining personal connections, and consistently exposing your child to rich language experiences, you're setting the stage for not just language proficiency, but a lifelong love of learning.

Every new word your child learns is a new tool for understanding and expressing themselves in the world. By supporting their vocabulary development, you're not just helping with language acquisition; you're expanding their ability to think, to connect, and to engage with the world around them. It's a gift that will serve them well throughout their lives, opening doors to academic success, cultural understanding, and global opportunities.

So embrace this journey of word discovery with your child. Make it a family adventure filled with curiosity, laughter, and the joy of shared learning. In doing so, you're not just building a vocabulary; you're crafting a legacy of language love that can last a lifetime.

- Chapter 11 -
DAILY ROUTINE IN HOW TO BE SUCCESSFUL LEARNING ENGLISH

The path to English proficiency is paved with daily habits and consistent practice. In my years of working with English language learners, I've observed that those who make the most progress are not necessarily the ones with the most innate linguistic talent, but rather those who approach their learning with dedication and integrate English into their daily lives. This chapter is dedicated to exploring how we can create a daily routine that fosters successful English language acquisition.

The Power of Routine in Language Learning

Routine is the backbone of effective learning. It provides structure, consistency, and a sense of progress that can be immensely motivating. When it comes to language learning, routine helps to create an immersive environment, even if you're not living in an English-speaking country. It's about making English a natural part of your day, rather than a separate task to be tackled.

The beauty of establishing a routine is that it reduces the mental effort required to engage with the language. When English practice becomes as automatic as brushing your teeth or eating breakfast, it ceases to feel like a chore. Instead, it becomes a seamless part of your day, something you do without question or hesitation.

Moreover, a well-structured routine allows for balanced practice across all language skills - listening, speaking, reading, and writing. It ensures that no aspect of language learning is neglected, leading to well-rounded proficiency.

But perhaps the most powerful aspect of routine in language learning is its cumulative effect. Small, consistent efforts compound over time, leading to significant progress. It's the linguistic equivalent of compound interest - every minute spent engaging with English adds up, creating a rich tapestry of language knowledge and skill.

Engaging Daily English Routine for Children

Creating an effective daily routine for children to learn English can transform language practice into an enjoyable part of their day. For children, interactive, playful approaches work best, especially when they involve parental participation. Start the day with some English songs or rhymes; this not only sets a positive tone but introduces new words in a catchy, memorable way. At breakfast, you can ask children to name foods in English or describe their morning plans, which builds vocabulary related to daily life.

Throughout the day, parents can incorporate English learning into play. For example, parents and children can create a 'word hunt' by finding objects around the home that match a list of English vocabulary words. Such games make language learning feel like an adventure and support vocabulary retention. If going to the grocery store or running errands, children can be encouraged to read out English words on labels or signs, giving them real-world exposure to the language.

In the evening, consider a short storytime where you read an English storybook together. Ask questions about the story to encourage comprehension and conversation. End the day with a reflection, where the child can share something they learned or an English word they found exciting. This makes language practice a warm, engaging ritual they look forward to.

Morning Rituals for English Immersion

The morning sets the tone for the entire day, making it an ideal time to immerse yourself in English. Here are some ways to infuse your morning routine with English language practice:

Start your day with English audio. Whether it's a podcast, an audiobook, or English language radio, let English be the first thing you hear in the morning. This could be while you're getting dressed, eating breakfast, or commuting to work or school. The key is to choose content that interests you - it could be news, storytelling, or discussions on topics you're passionate about.

Read something in English with your morning coffee or tea. This could be a news article, a chapter from an English book, or even social media posts in English. The goal is to engage with written English before your day gets busy.

Practice speaking English to yourself. This might feel awkward at first, but narrating your morning routine in English can be a powerful way to practice vocabulary and sentence structure. Describe what you're doing as you get ready for the day - "I'm brushing my teeth", "I'm choosing my clothes for today", etc.

Set a 'Word of the Day'. Choose a new English word each morning and challenge yourself to use it throughout the day. You could write it on a sticky note and place it somewhere visible, or set it as your phone's lock screen.

Write a short journal entry in English. This could be about your plans for the day, reflections on your dreams, or simply your current thoughts and feelings. The act of putting thoughts into written English helps solidify grammar and vocabulary.

Maximizing English Exposure Throughout the Day

The key to rapid progress in English is constant exposure and practice. Here are strategies to incorporate English into various aspects of your daily routine:

Change the language settings on your devices to English. This includes your phone, computer, and any apps you use regularly. This simple change can expose you to a wealth of everyday vocabulary.

Use English for practical tasks. When making a to-do list or shopping list, write it in English. If you use a calendar app, enter your appointments and reminders in English.

Take advantage of 'dead time'. Waiting in line, commuting, or doing household chores are all opportunities for English practice. Listen to English podcasts or audiobooks during these times.

For children or young learners, lunchtime can be a fun opportunity to interact with English in a relaxed, enjoyable setting. Parents can encourage children to describe their lunch in English, naming the colors, shapes, or tastes of the food. They can also play simple games, like "I Spy" using English words, or have the child tell a short story about their favorite food or a meal they've enjoyed. This approach makes lunchtime a playful way to practice vocabulary and conversational skills without feeling like a formal lesson.

Post-it note your surroundings. Label items around your home or workspace with their English names. This constant visual exposure can help reinforce vocabulary.

Think in English. Try to form your thoughts in English, even if you're not speaking out loud. This internal dialogue can be a powerful tool for improving fluency.

Evening Routines for Reflection and Consolidation with Children

The evening offers a calming time to reflect on the day and reinforce English learning. Parents can integrate English activities to help children process new vocabulary and phrases before bedtime in a relaxed setting.

Encourage children to revisit a 'Word of the Day' they learned, and help them come up with sentences using it. Watching an English-language cartoon or a short children's show together is also a great option. You can add English subtitles to support their understanding and discuss what they watched by asking questions about the characters or story.

Reading a bedtime story in English creates a cozy atmosphere while also building language skills. Choose a simple storybook and ask a few questions about the plot to spark curiosity and comprehension. For older children, have them write or draw about their day in an English journal. They can describe something fun they did or a new word they learned, giving them a sense of accomplishment.

To finish the day, play an English-language bedtime story or a relaxing guided meditation for children, allowing them to end the day with gentle English exposure as they fall asleep.

Weekends and Free Time: Balancing Structure and Fun for Young Learners

While routines are helpful, weekends are a great time for children to explore English in new and enjoyable ways. Parents can create opportunities for engaging, hands-on English activities that feel like fun rather than study.

Spend part of the weekend doing a family activity in English, like cooking a recipe together, where children can learn food-related vocabulary and follow simple instructions. You might also have an 'English Adventure Day'—visiting a park or local attraction and describing what you see in English, pretending to be a tour guide.

Encourage English-language hobbies. If your child enjoys art, try an English-language art tutorial. For children who like video games, some games can also support English vocabulary in a fun way, especially if played together.

A weekend English story or movie club can make English practice more social and collaborative. Choose a children's book or movie and discuss it as a family, or invite friends who are also learning English to join. Older children may also enjoy creating their content, such as drawing a comic in English or recording a simple video describing a hobby or adventure.

These activities allow children to practice English naturally while bonding with family and friends, keeping language learning both educational and exciting.

Adapting Your Routine for Different Life Stages and Circumstances

It's important to recognize that the ideal English learning routine will look different for everyone, depending on age, work or school commitments, family responsibilities, and personal preferences. The key is to find a routine that works for you and that you can stick to consistently.

For young learners, routines might involve more games, songs, and interactive activities. Teenagers might incorporate English into their social media use or hobbies. Working adults might focus on professional English and utilize commute times for learning.

If you have a busy schedule, focus on quality over quantity. Even 15 minutes of focused English practice each day can yield significant results over time. The key is consistency.

For those learning English as a family, create routines that involve everyone. This might include English dinner conversations, family game nights in English, or watching English movies together.

Be prepared to adjust your routine as your English skills improve or as your life circumstances change. What works for a beginner might not be challenging enough for an intermediate learner. Regular reassessment of your routine ensures that it continues to serve your learning needs.

Overcoming Challenges and Staying Motivated

Even with the best intentions, maintaining a daily English learning routine can be challenging. Here are some strategies for overcoming common obstacles:

If you miss a day, don't be discouraged. Simply pick up where you left off the next day. Consistency over time is more important than perfection.

If you're feeling bored with your routine, introduce new elements. Try a different podcast, switch to a new genre of books, or explore a new app for language learning.

Use technology to your advantage. Set reminders on your phone for different aspects of your English routine. Use apps that track your progress and provide motivation through streaks or achievements.

Find an accountability partner. This could be a friend, family member, or online language exchange partner. Regular check-ins can help keep you motivated and on track.

Celebrate your progress, no matter how small. Keep a record of new words learned, books read, or minutes spent practicing. Seeing your progress visually can be a powerful motivator.

The Long-Term View: Building a Lifestyle of English Learning

As you integrate these routines into your daily life, you'll find that English learning becomes less of a separate task and more a part of who you are. The goal is not just to learn English, but to live it.

Over time, these daily habits will compound, leading to significant improvements in your English proficiency. You may find yourself thinking in English, dreaming in English, and feeling more confident in English-speaking environments.

Remember that language learning is a journey, not a destination. There will always be new words to learn, new nuances to understand, and new ways to express yourself. Embrace this lifelong learning process and enjoy the endless discoveries that come with exploring a new language.

By creating and maintaining a daily routine for English learning, you're not just improving your language skills. You're opening doors to new opportunities, expanding your worldview, and enriching your life in countless ways. So embrace your daily English routine with enthusiasm and curiosity. Each day is a new chance to grow, to learn, and to connect with the wider English-speaking world.

The path to English proficiency is paved with daily steps. By weaving English into the fabric of your daily life through thoughtful routines and consistent practice, you create an immersive experience that accelerates your learning and makes the process more enjoyable. Whether you're a student, a professional, or a lifelong learner, these daily habits will serve as the foundation for your success in mastering the English language. So start today, be patient with yourself, and watch as your daily efforts bloom into English fluency.

Chapter 12

FUN ONE-TO-ONE ENGLISH TEACHING GAMES FOR PARENTS AND TEACHERS OF ESL

The journey of learning English can be transformed from a daunting task into an exciting adventure through the magic of play. In my years of experience teaching ESL, I've discovered that games are not just a break from 'real' learning – they are powerful tools that can accelerate language acquisition, boost confidence, and create lasting memories. This chapter is dedicated to exploring a variety of engaging, easy-to-implement games that parents and teachers can use in one-on-one settings to make English learning a joyful experience.

The Power of Play in Language Learning

Before we dive into specific games, it's crucial to understand why play is such a potent tool in language education. When we engage in play, our brains enter a state of relaxed alertness – the perfect condition for learning. The pressure to perform correctly diminishes, allowing learners to take risks with the language without fear of making mistakes. This freedom to experiment is essential for developing fluency and confidence in English.

Moreover, games provide context for language use, making abstract grammar rules and vocabulary come alive in meaningful ways. They create emotional connections to the learning material, which significantly enhances memory retention. The repetitive nature of many games also allows for natural reinforcement of language patterns without the tedium often associated with drills.

In one-on-one settings, games take on an even more powerful role. They create a bond between the teacher or parent and the learner, fostering a positive association with English learning. This personal connection can be a strong motivator for continued engagement with the language.

Vocabulary-Building Games

Expanding vocabulary is a cornerstone of language learning, and games can make this process both effective and enjoyable. Here are some games that focus on building and reinforcing vocabulary:

1. Word Basketball: Set up a small basket or container. Write vocabulary words on small pieces of paper. The learner picks a paper, reads the word aloud, uses it in a sentence, and then tries to toss it into the basket. If successful, they earn a point. This game combines physical activity with language practice, making it particularly effective for kinesthetic learners.

2. Pictionary with a Twist: Instead of drawing, use playdough or Lego to create representations of vocabulary words. This tactile approach can be especially engaging for younger learners or those who might be intimidated by drawing.

3. Word Chain: Start with a word and have the learner come up with another word that begins with the last letter of the previous word. For example: Cat – Tree – Elephant. This game reinforces spelling and encourages quick thinking in English.

4. Synonym Snap: Create cards with pairs of synonyms. Lay them face down and take turns flipping them over. When a matching pair is found, the first person to shout "Snap!" and use both words in a sentence wins the pair. This game not only builds vocabulary but also helps learners understand the nuances between similar words.

5. Category Race: Choose a category (e.g., animals, food, professions) and set a timer for one minute. See how many words in that category the learner can list. This game can be adapted for different proficiency levels by adjusting the categories and time limit.

Grammar Games

Grammar doesn't have to be dry or intimidating. These games make grammar practice interactive and fun:

1. Sentence Scramble: Write different parts of a sentence on separate cards (subject, verb, object, etc.). Mix them up and challenge the learner to arrange them into a correct

sentence. This hands-on approach helps learners visualize sentence structure.

2. Grammar Jenga: Write grammar questions or prompts on Jenga blocks. As each block is pulled, the player must answer the question or complete the prompt correctly. This adds an element of excitement to grammar practice.

3. Verb Charades: Act out different verbs and have the learner guess the action and then conjugate the verb in a specified tense. This game combines vocabulary, grammar, and physical activity.

4. Question Formation Race: Set a timer and see how many grammatically correct questions the learner can form in a given time. This game helps reinforce question structures, which are often challenging for ESL learners.

5. Error Correction Detective: Read a short paragraph with intentional grammar errors. Challenge the learner to be a "grammar detective" and spot and correct the mistakes. This game sharpens grammar awareness and editing skills.

Pronunciation and Speaking Games

Developing clear pronunciation and the confidence to speak are crucial aspects of English learning. These games focus on these important skills:

1. Tongue Twister Challenge: Start with simple tongue twisters and gradually increase difficulty. Time how long it takes to say them correctly three times in a row. This game not only

improves pronunciation but also brings a lot of laughter to the learning process.

2. Sound Sorting: Create cards with words that feature different phonetic sounds. Have the learner sort them into groups based on their pronunciation. This game helps learners recognize and differentiate between similar sounds in English.

3. Story Cube Narratives: Use story cubes (dice with pictures) to create impromptu stories. Roll the dice and create a story using the images that come up. This game encourages creative speaking and helps learners practice narrative tenses.

4. Mirror Talk: Sit face to face and have the learner mimic your mouth movements as you pronounce words or phrases. This visual approach can be particularly helpful for sounds that don't exist in the learner's native language.

5. Radio Show Role-play: Pretend to host a radio show together. This can involve weather reports, interviews, or storytelling segments. Role-play games like this help learners practice different speaking styles and registers.

Listening Comprehension Games

Developing strong listening skills is essential for overall language proficiency. These games make listening practice engaging and interactive:

1. Simon Says with a Twist: Play the classic game, but with more complex instructions that include prepositions,

adjectives, or specific vocabulary. For example, "Simon says touch something cylindrical in the room."

2. Song Gap-Fill: Play a familiar English song but pause it at certain points. The learner must remember and say the next word or phrase. This game combines listening skills with vocabulary recall.

3. Whisper Challenge: Whisper a phrase while the learner wears headphones playing music. They must try to understand what you're saying by reading your lips. This game sharpens both listening and visual comprehension skills.

4. Audio Treasure Hunt: Record clues that lead to hidden objects around the house or classroom. The learner must listen carefully to find each item. This game combines listening comprehension with following instructions in English.

5. Podcast Predictions: Listen to the beginning of a podcast episode together, then pause it and have the learner predict what will happen next. This game encourages active listening and speaking skills.

Reading and Writing Games

While often considered more solitary activities, reading and writing can be transformed into interactive games:

1. Story Continuation: Start a story with a single sentence. Take turns adding one sentence at a time to continue the

narrative. This game practices both reading comprehension and creative writing skills.

2. Speed Book Review: Set a timer for one minute. In that time, the learner must write as much as they can about a book they've read in English. This game practices quick recall and concise writing.
3. Alphabet Story: Create a story where each sentence begins with the next letter of the alphabet. This game challenges vocabulary recall and sentence formation skills.
4. Comic Strip Conversations: Use blank comic strip templates. One person writes dialogue for one character, and the other responds. This game practices both reading and writing in a visually engaging format.
5. Word Ladder: Start with a word and change one letter at a time to create new words, eventually reaching a target word. For example: Cat → Cot → Cog → Dog. This game combines spelling, vocabulary, and problem-solving skills.

Adapting Games for Different Proficiency Levels

The beauty of these games lies in their flexibility. They can be easily adapted to suit learners of different ages and proficiency levels.

Here are some tips for adaptation:

- For beginners, simplify the rules and focus on basic vocabulary and structures. Use more visual aids and physical actions to support understanding.

- For intermediate learners, increase the complexity of the language used in the games. Introduce time limits to challenge fluency and quick thinking in English.
- For advanced learners, incorporate more abstract concepts, idiomatic expressions, and complex grammatical structures into the games.
- Always be prepared to adjust the difficulty level during play. If a game is too easy, add additional challenges. If it's too difficult, provide more support or simplify certain aspects.

Creating a Positive Gaming Environment

The effectiveness of these games largely depends on the atmosphere in which they're played.

Here are some tips for creating a positive, encouraging environment:

- Emphasize fun over perfection. The goal is to engage with English, not to achieve flawless performance.
- Participate enthusiastically yourself. Your energy and excitement will be contagious.
- Offer praise for effort and improvement, not just correct answers.
- Use gentle error correction. Instead of pointing out mistakes directly, model the correct usage in your response.
- Allow for "think time." Don't rush to fill silences; give the learner time to process and formulate responses.

- Be flexible and responsive to the learner's mood and energy level. If a game isn't working, be willing to switch to something else.

Integrating Games into Regular Learning Routines

While games are fantastic learning tools, they're most effective when integrated thoughtfully into a broader learning strategy.

Here are some ideas for incorporating games into your regular English teaching routine:

- Use games as warm-up activities to get the learner engaged and thinking in English.
- Employ games as a way to review material covered in more formal lessons.
- Designate specific "game days" or times to give learners something to look forward to.
- Use games as rewards for completing other learning tasks.
- Create a "game menu" that the learner can choose from at the end of each lesson.

The Long-Term Impact of Game-Based Learning

As you incorporate these games into your English teaching, you'll likely notice benefits that extend far beyond language skills.

Game-based learning can:

- Boost confidence and willingness to take risks with the language.
- Improve problem-solving and critical thinking skills.
- Enhance social skills and emotional intelligence.
- Foster a lifelong love of learning and positive associations with English.
- Strengthen the bond between the teacher/parent and the learner.

Games are not just a fun addition to English learning – they are powerful tools that can transform the entire learning experience. By making play a central part of your ESL teaching approach, you're not just teaching English; you're creating an environment where language acquisition happens naturally and joyfully.

So, embrace the power of play in your English teaching. Experiment with these games, adapt them to your learner's needs, and don't be afraid to invent new ones. Remember, every moment of laughter, every burst of excitement, and every playful interaction is a step towards English proficiency. In the grand journey of language learning, these moments of joy are the fuel that keeps learners moving forward, eager to discover what new adventures await them in the world of English.

CONCLUSION

As we draw the curtains on this comprehensive guide, I find myself reflecting on the incredible journey we've embarked upon together. The path of English language acquisition is not a straight, paved road but rather a winding trail through a lush forest of knowledge, challenges, and discoveries. Each chapter of this book has been a stepping stone, guiding us through the intricacies of empowering English learners, and now, as we stand at the journey's end, we can look back with pride at the distance we've covered.

The Tapestry of ESL Education: Key Takeaways and Parental Involvement

Throughout this guide, we've woven together a rich tapestry of strategies, insights, and practical advice, all aimed at nurturing successful English language learners. At the heart of this tapestry lies a fundamental truth: the role of parents in ESL education is not just important – it's transformative.

One of the key takeaways that resonates throughout these pages is the power of creating an immersive English environment at home. We've explored how everyday moments – from dinner conversations to bedtime stories – can become opportunities for language learning. By infusing English into the fabric of daily life, parents create a seamless bridge between classroom learning and real-world application.

Another crucial thread in our tapestry is the emphasis on personalized learning strategies. We've delved into the myriad ways that different learners absorb language, from visual and auditory to kinesthetic approaches. By recognizing and catering to these individual learning styles, parents and teachers can unlock each child's unique potential for language acquisition.

The importance of emotional support in the language learning journey cannot be overstated. We've discussed how creating a safe, encouraging environment where mistakes are seen as stepping stones rather than stumbling blocks can dramatically boost a child's confidence and willingness to engage with English. This emotional scaffolding, primarily provided by parents, forms the foundation upon which all other learning strategies are built.

Technology, we've discovered, can be a powerful ally in ESL education when used judiciously. From language learning apps to educational videos, the digital world offers a wealth of resources that can complement traditional learning methods.

While balance is essential in screen time, virtual face-to-face platforms offer a unique opportunity for real-time language practice that feels interactive and personal. Through options like 1:1 sessions and small group classes, children and young learners can engage directly with teachers and peers, practicing English in a live, interactive environment. This approach combines the benefits of personalized instruction with the sense of connection that comes from face-to-face interaction, even in a digital format.

Such platforms can complement real-world activities by allowing children to practice conversational skills, pronunciation, and vocabulary in a supportive, virtual classroom setting. This method provides a bridge between structured learning and spontaneous, real-world language use, ensuring a well-rounded English learning experience.

The power of reading in English language acquisition has been a recurring theme. We've explored how shared reading experiences not only build vocabulary and comprehension skills but also foster a love for the language that can last a lifetime. Parents who make reading a daily ritual are gifting their children with far more than just language skills – they're opening doors to new worlds and perspectives.

Perhaps one of the most empowering takeaways has been the recognition that parents don't need to be English experts to support their child's learning effectively. We've shared numerous strategies for parents to engage in their child's ESL journey, regardless of their own English proficiency. From learning alongside their children to creating opportunities for authentic language use, parents have a toolkit of approaches to choose from.

The importance of cultural awareness and sensitivity in ESL education has been another key focus. We've discussed how language learning is intrinsically tied to cultural understanding, and how parents can play a vital role in helping their children navigate the cultural nuances of English-speaking communities while maintaining pride in their own cultural heritage.

The Ongoing Journey: Practicing English Together and Embracing Lifelong Learning

As we close this chapter of our ESL journey, it's crucial to recognize that the end of this book is not the end of the learning process. Language acquisition is a lifelong adventure, filled with continuous growth and discovery. The strategies and insights shared in these pages are not meant to be a finite set of instructions, but rather a springboard for ongoing exploration and practice.

I encourage parents and children to view English learning not as a task to be completed but as a shared adventure filled with exploration, connection, and growth. For teachers, this journey can also be transformative. Each class offers the chance to inspire and engage young learners, to create an environment where curiosity thrives, and confidence in language skills grows. By fostering a supportive space where children feel comfortable experimenting and making mistakes, teachers play a pivotal role in shaping a lifelong love for language learning.

Together, as teachers, parents, and students, we can approach English not just as a subject but as an experience that bridges cultures and brings families and communities closer. Let's embrace each milestone, cherish the small victories, and continue forward, making English learning a meaningful, joyful journey for everyone involved.

Consistency is key in language learning, and I urge families to make English practice a regular part of their routine. This doesn't mean setting aside hours each day for formal study – rather, it's about finding small, everyday opportunities to engage with the language. It could be as simple as having an "English hour" during dinner time, where the family challenges themselves to communicate only in English, or starting a tradition of writing weekly English journal entries together.

For children, the motivation to continue learning often comes from seeing the real-world applications of their skills. Parents can help by creating opportunities for their children to use English in authentic contexts – whether it's ordering at a restaurant, writing a letter to an English-speaking pen pal, or helping to plan a family trip to an English-speaking country. These experiences not only reinforce language skills but also demonstrate the practical value of English proficiency.

It's important to celebrate progress along the way, no matter how small. Keep track of milestones – the first time your child reads a book without translation, their first successful phone conversation in English, or the moment they understand a joke in an English TV show. These celebrations reinforce the joy of learning and provide motivation for continued effort.

As parents, one of the most powerful things you can do is model a love for learning. Share your own language learning experiences, challenges, and triumphs with your children. If you're learning English alongside them, be open about your own journey. This not only normalizes the learning process but also creates a shared experience that can bring you closer together.

Language learning is not a linear process. There will be plateaus and even moments of apparent regression. During these times, it's crucial to maintain a positive attitude and focus on the progress made rather than temporary setbacks. Every interaction with English, every attempt to use new vocabulary or grammar, is a step forward, even if it doesn't feel like it in the moment.

I also encourage families to seek out and create communities of fellow English learners. This could involve joining local ESL groups, participating in online forums, or organizing informal meetups with other families on similar language journeys. These communities can provide support, share resources, and offer opportunities for English practice in a supportive environment.

I urge parents and children alike to remain curious and open to the endless possibilities that English proficiency can bring. Whether it's accessing a wider range of educational opportunities, connecting with people from diverse backgrounds, or exploring global career paths, English skills open doors to a world of opportunities. By maintaining a mindset of lifelong learning, you're not just improving language skills – You're continually expanding your horizons and enriching life experiences for yourself and children.

A Note of Gratitude: Celebrating Your Commitment to the English Language Journey

As we come to the close of this guide, I want to express my deepest gratitude to you, the readers – the parents, teachers, and supporters who have dedicated yourselves to empowering English learners. Your commitment to this journey is nothing short of inspiring.

To the parents who have picked up this book, your dedication to your child's education is commendable. In a world that often moves too fast, you've chosen to invest time and effort into supporting your child's language learning journey. Your willingness to engage, to learn, and to create opportunities for English practice will have a profound impact on your child's future. The moments you spend reading together, practicing vocabulary, or simply conversing in English may seem small, but they are building blocks for your child's success and confidence.

To the teachers who have sought additional resources to support their students, your passion for education is evident. You understand that each child in your classroom is on a unique journey, and your efforts to personalize their learning experience can make all the difference. Your role extends far beyond teaching grammar and vocabulary – you are cultural bridges, confidence builders, and sometimes the first friendly face in a new and overwhelming environment. The impact you have on your students' lives extends far beyond the classroom walls.

To the English learners themselves, whether children or adults, your perseverance is admirable. Learning a new language is no small feat. It requires courage to make mistakes, resilience to keep trying, and an open mind to embrace new ways of thinking and expressing yourself. Every word you learn, every conversation you attempt, is a step towards your goals. Your willingness to embrace this challenge is a testament to your strength and determination.

I want to acknowledge that the ESL journey is not always easy. There are moments of frustration, times when progress seems slow, and challenges that may feel insurmountable. But it's precisely these moments that make the victories – no matter how small – so sweet. Each new word mastered, each successful conversation, each moment of understanding when watching an English movie without subtitles – these are triumphs worth celebrating.

Your dedication to this journey goes beyond personal or family benefit. In our increasingly interconnected world, English proficiency is a tool for building bridges between cultures, fostering global understanding, and creating opportunities for collaboration across borders. By supporting English language learners, you're contributing to a more connected, empathetic, and communicative global community.

As you continue on this language learning journey, I encourage you to be kind to yourselves. Celebrate your successes, learn from your challenges, and always remember why you started this journey. Whether it's for educational opportunities, career advancement, personal growth, or simply the joy of learning, hold onto that motivation.

Thank you for allowing me to be a part of your ESL journey through this book. It has been my privilege to share insights, strategies, and encouragement with you. While this book may be concluding, your journey with the English language is ongoing. May it continue to be filled with discoveries, connections, and moments of joy.

In closing, I want to leave you with this thought: Language learning is not just about mastering grammar rules or expanding vocabulary. It's about opening doors to new worlds, connecting with diverse people and cultures, and expanding your own capabilities. Every step you take on this journey, every effort you make to support an English learner, ripples out into the world, creating opportunities for understanding and connection.

Thank you for your dedication, your perseverance, and your commitment to empowering English learners. The impact of your efforts will be felt for generations to come. Keep learning, keep growing, and keep embracing the beautiful adventure that is language acquisition. The world is brighter because of your efforts to bridge linguistic and cultural divides. Here's to your continued success on this remarkable journey of English language learning!

Made in the USA
Columbia, SC
17 November 2024

407e5586-e31b-4e5d-b7f5-dc11fbd8f0b9R01